India

Third edition

Pamela Bhagat

First published by Oxfam GB in 2004

Available from:
Bournemouth English Book Centre, PO Box 1496, Parkstone, Dorset, BH12 3YD, UK
tel: +44 (0)1202 712933; fax: +44 (0)1202 712930;
email: oxfam@bebc.co.uk

USA: Stylus Publishing LLC, PO Box 605, Herndon, VA 20172-0605, USA
tel: +1 (0)703 661 1581; fax: +1 (0)703 661 1547;
email: styluspub@aol.com

For details of local agents and representatives in other countries, consult our website: www.oxfam.org.uk/publications or contact Oxfam Publishing, 274 Banbury Road, Oxford OX2 7DZ, UK
Tel: +44 (0)1865 311 311; fax: +44 (0)1865 312 600; email: publish@oxfam.org.uk

Our website contains a fully searchable database of all our titles, and facilities for secure on-line ordering.

Published by Oxfam GB, 274 Banbury Road, Oxford OX2 7DZ, UK.

Oxfam GB is a registered charity, no. 202 918, and is a member of Oxfam International.

© Oxfam GB 2004

ISBN 0 85598 495 3

A catalogue record for this publication is available from the British Library.

All rights reserved. Reproduction, copy, transmission, or translation of any part of this publication may be made only under the following conditions:
- with the prior written permission of the publisher; or
- with a licence from the Copyright Licensing Agency Ltd., 90 Tottenham Court Road, London W1P 9HE, UK, or from another national licensing agency; or
- for quotation in a review of the work; or
- under the terms set out below.

This publication is copyright, but may be reproduced by any method without fee for teaching purposes, but not for resale. Formal permission is required for all such uses, but normally will be granted immediately. For copying in any other circumstances, or for re-use in other publications, or for translation or adaptation, prior written permission must be obtained from the publisher, and a fee may be payable.

Printed by
    Information Press, Eynsham

Contents

Introduction 1

Five thousand years of history 3

Defining identities: religion, caste, and regional culture 14

A question of numbers 28

Economy and trade 34

India's untapped human potential 43

Out of the shadows: the place of women in Indian society 52

Rural livelihoods: claiming rights, protecting resources 62

Securing the future 77

Facts and figures 81

Dates and events 82

Sources and further reading 84

Acknowledgements 85

Oxfam GB in India 86

Index 88

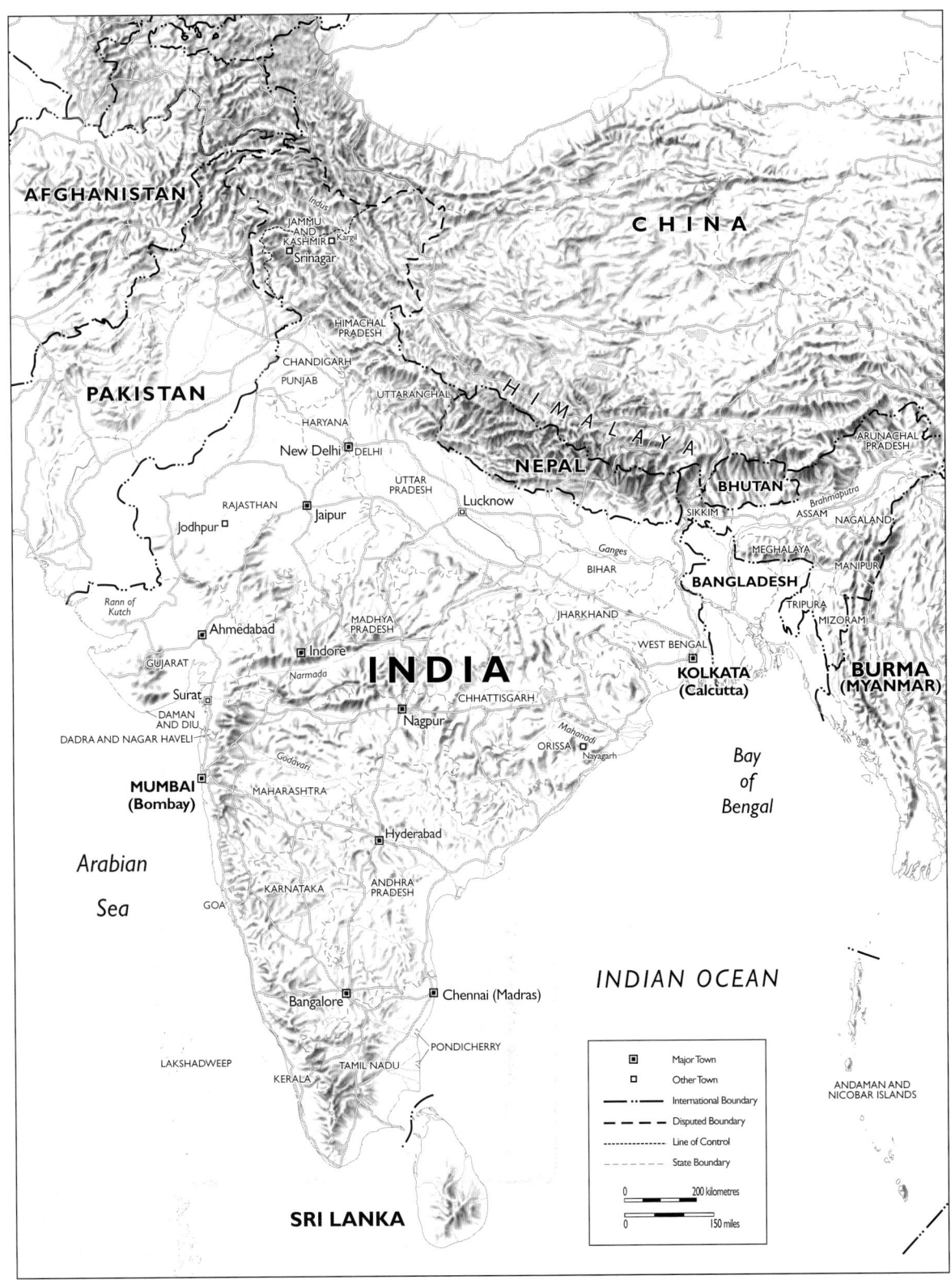

Introduction

India is a complex mosaic of ancient and modern elements. Traditional cultures exist side by side with sophisticated technologies. The mosaic contains 28 states, seven union territories, seven major religious communities, 18 official languages, and 1672 mother tongues. Until relatively recently, population movements from one region to another were limited, and as a result distinct regional cultures have evolved. Yet for travellers across India's enormous land mass, the absence of any sharp cultural boundaries creates a sense of smooth transition.

India's landscapes are very varied, ranging from the glacial Himalayas in the far north to the stark scrubland of Rajasthan in the west. There are the salt pans of Kutch and the tropical forests of Kerala. In the east are the mangrove swamps of the Sunderbans National Park in West Bengal and the evergreen forests of Assam. With this amazing diversity in habitats comes a remarkable richness of flora and fauna, giving India a wealth of wildlife.

The Indian subcontinent is extremely vulnerable to natural hazards. A weak summer monsoon means serious drought, poor crops, and famine. More than a quarter of India's land is prone to drought, affecting nearly 50 million people every year. More than one tenth of the land – a quarter of all arable land – is prone to flooding, especially in the Ganges and Brahmaputra basins, with consequent loss of lives and livelihoods.

◀ Map of India, showing states, union territories, and other places mentioned in this book

▶ Perambalur, Tamil Nadu: even in the smallest and most remote villages, satellite dishes are beginning to appear.

INDIA 1

India's long coastline of 7683 km is lashed by high-velocity winds, bringing cyclones of varying intensity to the south-eastern states. Earthquakes can strike terror and wreak destruction across more than half of the country.

India's history has been shaped by calamities and invasions, but the spirit of the nation is indomitable. Its defining characteristic is the resilience with which it absorbs new influences and evolves, rejecting all attempts at sudden and radical change.

The heart of the world's largest democracy is the capital, New Delhi, a modern city built on the site of seven ancient cities. The Republic Day Parade takes place on 26 January each year. There are impressive displays of technological advances and military strength, but there is also hype and hoopla: colourful folk dances to the beat of pulsating music, historical tableaux, and children's pageants. In 2001, as a weak winter sun appeared from behind the clouds, the President arrived in a resplendent horse-drawn carriage, preceded and followed by mounted cavalry. Soon there were deafening cheers from the excited crowds lining the flag-festooned route from Red Fort to Rajpath, the administrative centre of the city, as the phalanx of tableaux appeared.

Almost at that exact same moment and during just such a celebration, as schoolchildren marched around an unfurled tri-colour 1000 kilometres away, thousands of people perished in a devastating earthquake in Gujarat, a region forever associated with Mahatma Gandhi, 'the Father of the Nation'. Was the coincidence a case of collective *karma* – the consequence of negative actions in the past? Or was the earthquake destined to become just another memory in the national psyche? Religious or philosophical rationalisation was not even attempted. Rather, the region and the nation have repaired the damage and moved on – a sign of the ever-resilient, ever-evolving India.

Transient and eternal aspects of India:

▶ *a timeless statue of the Buddha*

▼ *a contemporary street scene in Chennai (formerly Madras)*

2 INDIA

Five thousand years of history

Mike Wells/Oxfam

The history of India can be traced back some 5000 years. Rich natural resources – spices, indigo, silk, sugar, saltpetre, sandalwood, and ivory – made it a target for invasion and colonisation by European powers from the fifteenth century AD onwards. But India's history of invasion reaches back to the Aryans, Indo-Europeans who came from the north-west and overthrew the great Dravidian city-based civilisation of Harappa in the valley of the Indus around 3000 BC. The hymns and poems of the Aryan Vedic culture are still recited in Hindu worship, giving India one of the oldest continuous cultural traditions in the world.

In the fifth century BC, Buddhism began to spread; it was embraced in the third century BC by the Mauryan emperor Ashoka, who controlled a greater proportion of India than any subsequent ruler until the Muslim emperors – the Mughals – more than 1000 years later.

Mighty empires and dynasties rose and fell after the collapse of the Mauryas, leaving behind them some of the great buildings and art of the world – the elaborately sculpted and painted caves of Ajanta, for example, created by the Gupta kings, whose empire was established in the third

▲ *The Konark Sun Temple, Orissa: built in 1250 AD in the shape of the chariot of the Sun God, drawn by exquisitely carved horses on huge stone wheels, representing the march of time.*

century AD, ushering in a golden age of poetry, literature, and art, during which Hinduism underwent a revival and Buddhism began to decline. The invasion of the Huns from the steppes of Central Asia in the fifth century signalled the end of the Gupta empire, which fragmented into a number of separate Hindu kingdoms.

From the eighth century AD onwards, Muslim invaders arrived from the Middle East, although it was not until 1192 that Islamic power arrived on a more permanent basis, when the first Sultan of Delhi established his court. In 1526, Babar, the first of the great Mughal emperors, arrived in the north-west from Turkey, defeated the Sultan, and established an empire that was to dominate north and central India until it waned in the eighteenth century – leaving a legacy of architecture, arts, and literature that still influences Indian culture today.

The far south of India was unaffected by the rise and fall of kingdoms in the north, and the status of Hinduism in this region was never challenged by Buddhism, or Jainism (a religion dating from the sixth century BC), or Islam. The prosperity of the south and its great empires was based on long-established trading links with Egypt, Rome, and South-East Asia.

Although peninsular India has a long coastline, it has never been a maritime nation; rather, it has had a continental mindset. It is a fact of history that invaders who came over land – Greeks, Persians, Arabs, Turks, Afghans, and Mughals – stayed on; but all invaders from the sea – the Dutch, Portuguese, French, and British – ultimately returned.

The jewel in the (British) crown

British power in India was initially exercised by the East India Company, which established a trading post at Surat in Gujarat in 1612. The British were not the first or the only European power with a presence in India in the seventeenth century: the Portuguese had been in control in Cochin since 1503 (before the Mughals arrived), and the French and Dutch also had trading posts. After the Battle of Plassey in 1757, when Robert Clive, Governor General of Bengal, recaptured Calcutta from the *nawab* of Bengal, Siraj-ud-Daula, the power of Britain gradually spread until conclusively demonstrated by victory in the fourth Mysore War in 1799. The long-running British struggle with the Marathas was concluded in 1818, leaving almost the entire country under the control of the British East India Company.

The colonisers regarded India as a place to make money; they did not seek to interfere with its culture, beliefs, and religions. The British expanded iron and coal mining, developed tea, coffee, and cotton plantations, and

▼ *The Victoria Memorial in Kolkata, opened by the Prince of Wales in 1921. The park is a popular place for picnics.*

began construction of India's vast rail network. They encouraged the system of absentee landlords, because it made administration and tax collection easier, but in the process they created an impoverished and landless peasantry – a problem which persists in several regions, especially Bihar and West Bengal, even today. An uprising in northern India in 1857 (referred to as 'the First War of Independence' by Indians and as 'the Sepoy Mutiny' by the British) led to the demise of the East India Company, and administration of the country was taken over by the Crown. In the next 50 years, the British empire in India expanded its dominion and exploited the country's resources for its own industries at home. But resentment against this policy was growing ...

Moves towards self-rule

Opposition to British rule began in earnest at the turn of the twentieth century. Until then, from the very first meeting of nominated members in 1885, the Indian National Congress had been resorting to 'petition, prayer, and protest' to achieve greater power for Indians in legislative councils, and to challenge imperialist exploitation of the country's resources.
The Congress now began to push for *swaraj* – self-rule. Outside Congress, hot-blooded individuals pressed for independence by more violent means. In 1915 a young lawyer, Mohandas Karamchand Gandhi, returned home from South Africa. His policy of non-violent resistance – *satyagraha* – to British rule soon became the defining feature of India's independence movement.

World War II brought the end of imperialism, and Indian independence became inevitable. However, local elections began to reveal the alarming growth of communalism, with the Muslim League, led by Muhammed Ali Jinnah, speaking for the majority of Muslims, and the Congress Party, led by Jawaharlal Nehru, representing the Hindu population. An overwhelming number of Indian Muslims began demanding a separate homeland.

Prompted by rising political and communal tension, the British government decided to divide the country, and the Viceroy, Lord Mountbatten, set a rapid timetable for independence. Unfortunately, the two predominantly Muslim regions were on opposite sides of the country, meaning that the new nation of Pakistan would consist of two halves, East and West, divided by India. When the dividing line was announced, the greatest violent exodus in human history took place, as Muslims moved to Pakistan, and Hindus and Sikhs relocated to India. More than 10 million people changed sides, and 250,000 people (a conservative estimate) were slaughtered in mindless barbaric violence.

In the final stages of the independence campaign there was one last tragedy to be played out. On 30 January 1948 Gandhi, deeply saddened by the partition of the nation and the subsequent bloodshed, was assassinated by a Hindu fanatic.

▲ *Rajiv Gandhi was the driving force behind the construction of India's national telephone network. Even the smallest village has at least one public booth, enabling families all over India to keep in touch with each other.*

Independence and after

Following the trauma of partition, India's first prime minister, Jawaharlal Nehru, championed a secular constitution, socialist central planning, and a strict policy of non-alignment in foreign affairs. The India of today is vastly different from that of the late 1940s, when the constitution was framed. Since 1947 and through 13 general elections, democratic institutions have been strengthened, the size of the population has more than doubled, social tensions have increased, and political fragmentation has occurred – but Indian democracy continues to function.

The fulfilment of India's 'tryst with destiny' (to quote Nehru's commemorative speech on Independence Day) at midnight on 15 August 1947 was the beginning of a long political journey. India has maintained cordial relations with its former colonisers and elected to join the Commonwealth. Continuing the domination of domestic politics by the Congress Party, Nehru's daughter Indira Gandhi became Prime Minister in 1966. After she was assassinated in 1984, the Gandhi dynasty's grip on Indian politics continued when the party brought in her son, Rajiv Gandhi. Best known for his attempts to propel India into the world's economy, he suffered a fate similar to his mother's when he was assassinated during an election campaign in 1991.

Since then India has experienced numerous political mutations, and coalition politics has become the norm. Increasing political awareness among the public has led to the emergence of a multi-party system. Today there are as many as seven national political parties and 38 regional parties registered with the Election Commission, many of them representing factions based on cultural, social, ethnic, caste, community, and religious interests.

Coalition governments can confer indirect advantages, such as a wider representation of views, and greater consensus on significant issues. Also they reduce the possibility of a party with an overwhelming majority imposing a state of emergency like the one declared by Indira Gandhi in 1975, which was accompanied by draconian laws and infringements of civil liberties. At the same time, coalition governments can create political instability, giving rise to dangerously divisive communal politics.

Religious differences have not always led to conflict and violence in India: communities of different faiths have co-existed peacefully for years, and continue to do so in many parts of the country. But, for historical reasons, communalism is deep-rooted in the Hindu psyche, and the emotional insecurity of voters who perceive traditional values to be threatened by the advance of a 'modern' or different culture can be exploited by politicians all too easily. These dangers were clearly evident during the violent conflict at

▶ *Kolkata: catching up on the news. In addition to national newspapers – The Times of India, The Hindustan Times, The Statesman, and Indian Express – most major cities also have their own newspapers.*

Ayodhya in 1992, when a Hindu mob stormed and destroyed a mosque which they believed had been built on the legendary site of the birth of Lord Rama, the seventh incarnation of the Hindu deity Vishnu.

Playing on the national sense of insecurity, in 1998 the BJP government (formed by the *Bhartiya Janata Party*, whose policies are inspired by Hindu nationalism) fulfilled its promise to make India a nuclear weapons state. Despite international outrage, the nuclear tests were met with widespread jubilation in India and created a groundswell of support for the BJP. The elections held in 1999 produced the NDA (National Democratic Alliance) government, a 22-party coalition led by BJP's Atal Behari Vajpayee. This government was able to function partly on the strength of its pragmatic survival instincts and partly also because of the failure of opposing parties to unite to defeat it.

Yet, against all expectations, the elections for the *Lok Sabha* (lower house) held in 2004 decisively voted out the ruling BJP. Although Sonia Gandhi, the Italian widow of Rajiv Gandhi, led the Congress Party's winning campaign, she declined to accept the most powerful job in the country. Manmohan Singh, a renowned economist, was sworn in as prime minister, heading a 19-party coalition – the United Progressive Alliance – which includes parties of the left.

It is now generally accepted that only coalition politics can accommodate the intrinsic diversity of this complex nation. By and large, the constitution of India has tried to meet the demands and aspirations of the people, within the framework and through the mechanisms provided, even though India continues to face major social, economic, and political challenges.

Independence for women?

Independence for India did not automatically mean freedom for women. Mahatma Gandhi's mass mobilisation for self-rule had involved women from all sections of society and leaders of the women's movement, as it then existed; and it had international links with the suffragettes and the anti-imperialist movements of the West. But only a small minority of women were active in the movement for independence. For the majority, life was a daily struggle for survival: barely 7 per cent were literate; female life expectancy was a mere 37 years; and maternal mortality was as high as 100 per 1000 cases of childbirth.

In the early years after independence, government planners tended to perceive women as weak, disadvantaged, and in need of welfare provision. In the 1970s and 1980s, more constructive ideas about social development came to the fore; and in the 1990s the goal became women's empowerment.

▼ The poster, produced by students in Lucknow, says: 'Sexual harassment makes it hard for girls to leave their homes. Is this proper?'

Shalan Parker/Oxfam

The past half-century has witnessed changes in the status of women, in terms of their health, literacy, employment, and political and civil rights. Some political decisions now have to take account of women's concerns. Women are becoming more aware of their rights and are willing to assert them. In the fields of business, medicine, engineering, law, art, and culture, they are making major contributions. Yet, while some women are emerging strong and confident, in control of their lives, the majority still have to contend with a very different reality.

Most Indian women are far from enjoying equal status with men, whether in terms of equality before the law, in marriage, in the family, or in the wider society. The constitution guarantees equality for all, but the laws that have been passed to improve the lot of women are not widely implemented. There is a lack of will to do so among politicians, judges, the police, and, ultimately, men in general.

The structures of democracy

Independent India opted for a federal structure with a strong union. Administration, public welfare, and development are the responsibility of the individual states, but from the beginning taxes and other revenues have been collected centrally, in an attempt to achieve the social objectives of the whole nation: the alleviation of poverty, and the promotion of equality in development. But in reality states and central governments are often run by different – and opposing – political parties. The exercise of the presidential power to dismiss state governments and to assume control of state

INDIA 9

administration is the subject of much controversy, because it has been imposed on several occasions for partisan purposes.

In several states, including Punjab, Kashmir, Assam, and Nagaland, conflict over development policies, the displacement of communities by destructive environmental schemes, violations of civil liberties, insensitive economic policies and reforms, and the exploitation of rural areas by the urban classes have led to terrorism and militant armed conflict directed against the Indian nation-state. Such tensions in the relationship between central government and individual states have created a demand for greater devolution of power, and for local control over natural resources.

After independence, enormous power and resources became concentrated in the hands of the bureaucracy, under its socialist political masters. Governance, good or bad, depends on the political parties, personalities, administration, and institutions provided for it, and in the current Indian scene the politicisation of administrative institutions has created overlapping spheres of control. This has brought into sharp focus the inadequacy of the bureaucracy, which was once perceived to be 'the steel frame of India's democracy'.

The professional civil service that India inherited from the colonial period was created to maintain law and order, collect revenues, administer justice, and maintain the communications system. It had limited experience of development work. After independence, there was a vast expansion of civil and technical services, which created major problems of co-ordination and management and led to delay and inefficiency. In addition, there is growing evidence of unwarranted political interference, corruption, and inadequate leadership at all levels of the civil service. The administrative apparatus built for sustaining colonial rule is inadequate for totally different priorities in an independent country. A vast system of state-level licences and quotas, commonly referred to as *'the licence raj'*, is blamed by many observers for distortions in development and economic growth which prevent India from exploiting its potential in the modern globalised world.

The concept of the separation of power between the executive, the legislature, and the judiciary is built into India's constitution. While the judiciary has played a positive role in safeguarding civil rights and has been vigilant in preserving the spirit of the constitution against legislative and executive intrusions, it has not been very successful in providing justice for private citizens. Partly due to a huge backlog of cases, and due also to the fact that the judiciary seems to be more responsive to the demands of the Bar than to the needs of the client, ordinary people are losing faith in the judicial system. There is an urgent need for a less formal system of adjudication, the establishment of *Lok Adalats* (people's courts), and a revival of village courts to reduce the burden on the judicial system and also to make justice more affordable and more expeditious.

Grassroots governance

Gandhi's remark that India lives in the villages is still relevant, since three-quarters of the population continue to live in rural areas, spread over 600,000 villages. In a country where 26 per cent of the people live below the official poverty line and millions are unemployed or underemployed, improving conditions in these deprived areas should be the main objective of rural development.

It was to address this need that the constitution was amended by the 73rd and 74th Amendments Act in 1992, with the aim of strengthening and revitalising the existing system of local governance known as *Panchayati Raj Institutions* (PRIs). These constitutional safeguards against interference from the bureaucracy and politicians should enable the common people to decide and implement their own development priorities. The PRI structure has three tiers: the village *panchayat*, the block *panchayat* (also called *taluk* or *mandal*), and the district *panchayat*, all consisting of elected representatives of the people. At present some two million *panchayats* at the village level, 6000 at the intermediate level, and another 474 at the district level are estimated to be functioning.

The *panchayats* are responsible for 29 aspects of local development, including agriculture, minor irrigation schemes, water management, primary and secondary schools, health care, and maintenance of the community's natural resources, including common assets. At each of the three levels there are reservations for scheduled castes and tribes (traditionally excluded from mainstream society), in proportion to their numbers in the local population. A distinctive feature of this Act is that one-third of the seats are reserved for women. These reservations extend to the post of chairperson of a *panchayat*.

▼ *A village elder has his say at a meeting in Gujarat.*

The results of the reforms have been mixed. In some areas, vested political interests have tried to subvert the PRIs: for instance, while it is mandatory to hold elections once every five years, many states have succeeded in circumventing this provision; some have set up parallel bodies to implement programmes; most have transferred only limited funds and functionaries to PRIs. While Kerala, Karnataka, and four other states have transferred all 29 prescribed responsibilities to the PRIs, only Karnataka has transferred both funds and functionaries. Central government is guilty of diverting funds for rural schemes through the District Rural Development Agencies, rather than channelling them directly to PRIs.

At the level of elected members too there are variations. In Kerala, where there is a dominant political party and political divisions are not overpowering, there have been success stories. Areas with well-established tribal societies, such as Arunachal Pradesh and other eastern states, have achieved a large measure of success through their traditional organisations of local self-government. But in other regions, there is a need for elected members – particularly women – to be given training to enable them to be effective agents of change. The government needs to work through and support NGOs, women's groups, and grassroots organisations to complement the initiatives taken by local governing bodies.

Although PRIs had been in existence since 1952, their potential for local democracy was not developed until recently. Now there is a growing recognition of the fact that little can be done to improve the prospects of the poor if they are isolated from the processes that shape their lives. But it remains to be seen whether official intentions and rhetorical resolutions will eventually be translated into actual empowerment of PRIs.

Regional dynamics in South Asia

South Asia is an ancient crucible of civilisations in which people and their cultures and religions are inextricably intermixed. India shares boundaries with five of the six countries in the region, and so is subject to illegal migration and drug trafficking. Borders in this region cut across communities, so that domestic crises tend to spread across frontiers. Millions of Bengalis in former East Pakistan fled to India in 1971. Since the mid-1990s, Chakmas from the Chittagong Hill tracts in Bangladesh have sought asylum in India. Similarly, dissidents from Punjab and Kashmir have sought asylum in neighbouring Pakistan.

Most of India's border regions, except Punjab, are under-developed. They are physically isolated, mainly because transport and communications are poor. They are also culturally different from the core of the Indian Union. All this contributes to a sense of alienation among the border people. These areas are complex to manage and are subject to insurgency, terrorism, and hostility from neighbours. A number of bilateral disputes in South Asia affect these populations, and many families are divided across borders. While some of the disputes are rooted in the historical past, others are a consequence of the current dynamics of bilateral and international relations.

The question of Kashmir

Islam came to Kashmir in the thirteenth century AD, and the region became a province of the Mughal empire in 1586. In the eighteenth century it was incorporated into the Afghan empire and was ruled by a string of Afghan governors who were renowned for their cruelty towards the Hindus. In 1819, Kashmir passed into the control of Sikh rulers, who proceeded to exploit the region; a severe famine reduced its population from 800,000 to 200,000. The British detached Kashmir from the Sikh kingdom in 1846 and handed the territory to the Hindu *raja* of Jammu for a sum of money, while retaining their supremacy over the newly created princely state of Jammu and Kashmir. Among the 565 princely states of British India, Kashmir was unique: it had a large Muslim majority population but was ruled by a Hindu monarch; and it bordered both India and the future Pakistan.

After the partition, Kashmir was given the choice of joining either India or Pakistan. Maharaja Hari Singh refused to accede to either country. He had grander plans: he wanted independence. But in October 1947, after an armed attack from Pakistan, he appealed to India for military assistance and then acceded to India. The Indian troops stopped the Pakistani onslaught on Kashmir, but by then the infiltrators had captured one third of the former princely state. Fighting between India and Pakistan continued in Kashmir until the United Nations imposed a ceasefire in January 1949, and a ceasefire line was established that divided Kashmir between the two neighbours.

▲ *Conditions in India's northern border regions are harsh and inhospitable.*

1987 was a turning point in Kashmir's recent history. Widespread fraud and corruption characterised the state elections in that year, alienating ordinary Kashmiris and increasing their sense of grievance against India. The government that came to power in Jammu and Kashmir lacked legitimacy. Protests and demonstrations throughout the state became violent and took on a secessionist tenor.

In the summer of 1999, Pakistan crossed the ceasefire line (renamed the Line of Control and ratified by both countries under the Simla Agreement in 1972) with a deep incursion into remote, mountainous territory under Indian authority. The result was the Kargil War – brief but potentially serious, as both countries now possessed (and had tested) nuclear weapons.

The new government in Delhi is maintaining the policy of the previous administration in seeking a political solution to the crisis. While official talks continue between the foreign ministers of India and Pakistan, the peace process is also moving forward, in the form of cultural and diplomatic exchanges, and improved transport and communications links.

Defining identities: religion, caste, and regional culture

Independent India was born at a time of intense sectarian strife and human tragedy. It was in this context that the Indian State had to design an instrument which would protect its citizens from the forces of religious fundamentalism. Accordingly, the constitution proclaimed India to be a Sovereign Socialist Secular Democratic Republic.

Mahatma Gandhi defined secularism as *Sarva Dharma Sambhava* ('able to co-exist with all religions'); Jawaharlal Nehru defined it as *Dharma Nirpekshata* ('unrelated to affairs of religion'). The Indian constitution has tried to reconcile an insistence on secularism in public life with individual freedom of religion. The freedoms to profess, practise, and propagate religion are fundamental rights of all Indian citizens. The nation is expected to show equal respect for all religions, faiths, and modes of worship and to give them equal protection under the law. Although Hindus constitute 85 per cent of the population, in law Hinduism is regarded not as the principal religion, but only as the majority religion.

Because different faiths, communities, and castes have evolved and merged to shape Indian culture, secularism was seen as a condition necessary for social unity. However, in the past 30 years there has been increasing evidence of political parties resorting to non-secular politics for electoral gains, in violation of the Representation of the People Act, which prohibits the use of religion or caste in politics.

Unlike Europe, where religious denominations have wielded political power, India has no such tradition. There are hardly any instances of religious leaders insisting on making politics subservient to religion. On the contrary, it is the politicians who have attempted to take over religious institutions and destroy their sanctity. One could say that it is not politics that needs saving from religion, but religion and the secular credentials of the country that need to be protected from politicians.

A question of faith

Religion forms a crucial aspect of identity for most Indians, and much of India's history can be understood in terms of the interplay among its diverse religious groups. Hinduism, a collection of diverse doctrines and sects, is a

▲ The Sriranganathsvami Temple, Tamil Nadu, dedicated to the Hindu god Vishnu. In one corner of its 'thousand pillar hall' there is a shrine to Tulukka Nachiyar, the god's Muslim consort.

way of life followed by the majority of the population. It is the largest religion in Asia, and one of the world's oldest extant faiths (pre-dating history). Hinduism does not proselytise, since one can only be born into it, not convert to it.

Buddhism, founded in northern India in about 500 BC, spread rapidly after Emperor Ashoka embraced it in 261 BC. Hindus regard Buddha as another incarnation of their god Vishnu. There are 6.6 million Buddhists in India, mainly concentrated in Sikkim, Arunachal Pradesh, and Jammu and Kashmir. The Jain religion was established in the sixth century BC as an attempt to reform brahminical Hinduism, with its upper-caste monopoly on knowledge, wealth, and power. Jainism emerged at around the same time as Buddhism, but did not find adherents outside India. It is most prominent in Maharashtra, Gujarat, and Rajasthan.

India's Muslim population is one of the largest in the world, numbering 130 million. The faith of the Prophet was first brought to the sub-continent by invaders in the eighth century AD. Among Indian Muslims, Sunnis are the majority sect. There are, however, influential Shi'ite trading communities in Gujarat – Khojas and Bohras – and Shi'ite aristocrats of Persian origin in Lucknow and Hyderabad. Muslim influence is particularly strong and visible in architecture, art, and traditional cuisine.

The Sikhs in India, numbering 18 million, mostly live in Punjab. Their religion (founded by Guru Nanak, 1469–1538) was originally intended to bring together the best of Hinduism and Islam. Its basic tenets are similar to those of Hinduism, with the important exception that the Sikhs are opposed to caste distinctions. The holiest shrine of the Sikh religion is the Golden Temple in Amritsar.

Roman Catholics form the largest single Christian group, especially in the western coastal areas and in southern India. Converts to Christianity, especially since the mid-nineteenth century, are largely from the disadvantaged castes and tribal groups. Other religious minorities in India include some communities of Jews; Zoroastrians, who wield influence out of all proportion to their small numbers; and Tribals, who constitute eight per cent of the Indian population and practise various forms of animism, which is perhaps the country's oldest religious tradition.

Hindus are in the majority in every Indian state except Jammu and Kashmir (two-thirds Muslims), Punjab (three-fifths Sikh), Meghalaya, Mizoram, and Nagaland (mainly Christian), and Arunachal Pradesh (predominantly Animist). Hindus also form the majority in five of the seven union territories (directly administered by central government), except Lakshadweep, which is more than 90 per cent Muslim.

The Hindu religion has proved to be a very powerful assimilating force. Popular religious expression is often local in character and crosses the boundaries of different faiths. For example, in Kerala Hindus, Muslims, and Christians alike practise the tradition of offering flowers and fruits at the altar, and married women's custom of wearing a necklace of black beads and gold to signify their marital status. Sadly, in the political climate that has recently and rapidly developed, religious faith is now being polarised, and the dominance of Hinduism causes friction, expressed in various forms. On a sub-continental scale, the major communal difference is between Hindus and Muslims. This legacy of partition has been accentuated by the post-colonial political atmosphere of India.

The politicisation of religion

The rich diversity of Indian society, which in previous decades has been contained in the secular State, is increasingly mutating towards regionalism (and even sub-regionalism), and communal conflicts based on religion, caste, and language. In a society that is still deeply religious in the traditional sense, passions can be aroused and exploited on highly sensitive issues. Fanaticism is contributing to a steady increase in the frequency of communal conflicts, with many people killed and injured as a result. Though precise and credible numbers are difficult to obtain, because of the disparities between government figures and independent estimates, it is certain that the resultant suffering affects members of all castes and religions.

Sohail (see box below) is a victim of communal violence that rocked Ahmedabad, Gujarat's biggest city, in 2002. This was not the first time that Ahmedabad had suffered communal tensions. Violence in the city followed the destruction of the Babri Mosque at Ayodhya in Uttar Pradesh by Hindu extremists in 1992, and the spill-over from the intense rioting that ensued in Mumbai in 1993.

A CHILD'S VIEW OF COMMUNAL TENSIONS

Eleven-year-old Sohail says, 'I once owned a football, but I lost it when our house was torched by a mob on 28 February 2002.' Along with four truckloads of their neighbours, Sohail's family managed to escape from Patia to an exclusively Muslim enclave – Juhapura, in Ahmedabad. 'I saw very bad people killing my neighbours. My brother Asif and sister Najo are both physically handicapped and they lost their wheelchairs. *Ammi* [mother] cries all the time because *Abu* [father] lost his job. I lost my football, but I don't cry. A *sanstha* [organisation – the Gujarat Sarvajanik Relief Committee] helped us to get a house and a bicycle so that I could ferry my brother and sister to school. In the afternoons I work hard at *bharat bharna* [machine embroidery] to supplement our family income. My favourite subjects have always been science and Hindi, but now my teachers insist that Urdu is more important for Muslims.'

HINDUS HOMELESS IN JAMMU

Neerja Kaul's circumstances have been reduced from a genteel urban life to an existence of penury in a ghetto in Jammu. It was in 1989 that she and her family – husband, father-in-law, and three children – left Srinagar in Kashmir under threat from Muslim extremists, never to return.

'Initially, when militancy began, we thought of staying and braving it out, but with Kashmiri Pandits [the Hindu community of Kashmir] being increasingly targeted, our resolve evaporated. After 20 years, insecurity and anger persist. Are we going to be homeless for ever?'

A FATEFUL NIGHT FOR MUSLIMS IN GUJARAT

Mehmoodaben has a haunted look as she huddles in the burnt-out shell of her house with mother-in-law Jeeviben, sister-in-law Madinaben, husband Rajak Bhai, and seven children. They have just returned to Navarevas (north Gujarat), after taking refuge for more than a year in Sabli camp, an encampment for victims of communal violence in Ahmedabad. 'It was our neighbours who attacked us, but also neighbours who saved us by unlocking the door for us to escape that fateful night. Oxfam is helping us to rebuild our house and has also replaced my husband's burnt-out shack, from which he used to sell vegetables. But the situation is different now. He is not being allowed to operate from the same place as before.'

Communal riots in one state have often spread to others, and even across the borders to neighbouring countries in South Asia. After the bloodshed of partition in 1947, the first major conflicts between Hindus and Muslims occurred in Jabalpur in the central Indian state of Madhya Pradesh in 1961. This was followed by riots in the northern state of Uttar Pradesh. Consequently, when Mehmoodaben is attacked in Gujarat, Hindus are victimised in Bangladesh; when Neerja Kaul suffers in Jammu and Kashmir, Muslims are punished in Uttar Pradesh, and minority communities such as Christians and Bengalis are socially and economically marginalised in Pakistan.

Contemporary communalism in India is a specific political ideology which exploits both religious identities and secular democratic opportunities, such as multi-party elections, in order to capture political power. The result is not so much the injection of religious fundamentalism into politics, but the transformation of a religious community into a political and electoral community. Hindu revivalism is intended to achieve this end, but it is 'justified' as a reaction to Islamic resurgence and to the government's perceived appeasement of the minorities.

India's complex polity consists of a range of constituencies with cross-cutting interests: linguistic or caste affinities, for example, often supersede religious loyalty. Hindu nationalism is therefore unlikely to become a cohesive force throughout the country. Besides, since Independence, India's leaders have been responsive to the claims of diverse ethnic groups and minorities. In the first 15 years, eleven new states were created, shaped by linguistic and cultural identities. Apart from this there are institutions such as the National Commission for Minorities and the National Integration Council, founded on the premise that traditional values which conflict with basic human rights cannot be respected and should not be tolerated on any grounds.

While the heritage of an ancient civilisation provides the roots and strength of the nation, what Sohail, Neerja Kaul, and Mehmoodaben experience today has to be assessed not in relation to India's glorious past, but in terms of the agenda that India has laid down for itself as a secular nation-state.

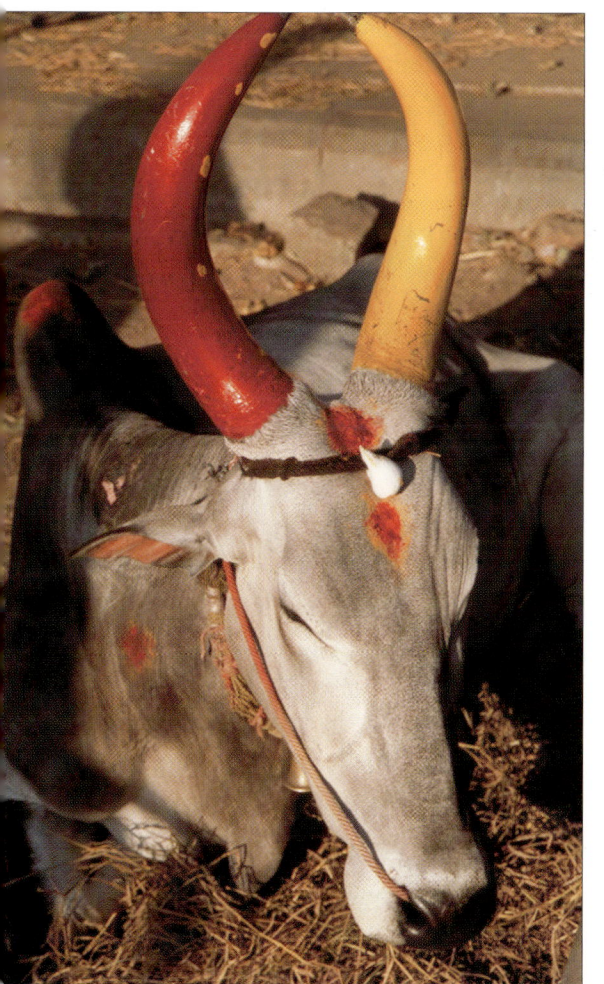

▼ *Throughout India, cows and bulls are venerated as sacred animals. Decorated with flowers and trinkets, their horns often brightly painted, they roam freely.*

Shailan Parker/Oxfam

Caste: caught in the web

Equally destructive are the social divisions based on caste. The caste system, which has been an integral part of the Hindu social structure for centuries, has played a major role in the evolution of Indian society. The division of people into various castes resulted in rigid social stratification. The hierarchical nature of the stratification enabled the higher castes to exploit the lower ones, claiming divine sanction for their privileged social status.

The most damaging impact of the caste system is not so much the supremacy of the upper castes as the conditioning of the lower castes to accept their inferior status as part of the natural order of things. No social institution characterised by so large an element of inequality and discrimination against a majority of the people can survive so long in a purely social context. It was through an elaborate, complex, and subtle scheme of scripture, mythology, and ritual that the caste system was invested with a moral authority that has seldom been effectively challenged, even by the most ardent social reformer.

This scheme of social organisation, which has survived for more than three thousand years, had far-reaching effects on the growth and development of various communities. For instance, as exclusive custodians of higher knowledge, the *brahmins* developed into a highly cultivated community with

INDIA 19

A Victory for Dalits at the Barber's

Until a year ago, 30-year-old Bhuplal had never travelled beyond the desert village of Bavri in Jodhpur District, Rajasthan. 'It was an area of darkness in this age of awareness. Upper-caste people did not allow us to wear coloured turbans or ride bicycles, and we had to remove our footwear in their presence. Any deviation from these practices was a licence for atrocities like public beating and humiliation. The local barbers refused to serve *dalits* [tribal people] and they would never cut our hair. Discrimination in public places was common and accepted – until we came in contact with an organisation called *Dalit Adhikar Abhiyan*, in 2001. We raised the issue of discrimination by barbers. The organisation helped us to contact the state officials in Jodhpur. The whole community joined forces and took up the issue through the Scheduled Castes and Scheduled Tribes (Prevention of Atrocities) Act. The barbers ultimately succumbed to our collective pressure and not only apologised but dedicated a whole day to our service. Now things are dramatically different in our village – but not in neighbouring villages.'

a special flair for intellectual pursuits. On the other hand, the *sudras*, continuously subjected to all sorts of deprivation, acquired all the traits of illiterate rustics. In traditional Indian society, social deprivation was a direct consequence of caste status, and various other types of discrimination arose directly from this pernicious system.

The superior position of the upper castes in Indian society was strengthened during the early years of British rule, when Western education further enhanced their social and economic status. During the freedom struggle, however, inspired by the best of Indian values, the fight against colonialism, the influences of Western liberal thought, and the ideals of socialism, Indian leaders felt an imperative need to create an egalitarian society. The spread of nationalism cut across the boundaries of caste, class, and religion.

The constitution, adopted in 1950, recognised the caste system as a source of inequity in Indian society and made provisions for affirmative action in favour of deprived groups. Reservation for the Scheduled Castes, Scheduled Tribes, and 'Other Backward Classes' was provided for in government jobs, professional appointments, and educational institutions. Apart from being a means of social and economic advance, reservation was seen as a way of ensuring the representation of the interests of these groups in the governance of the country.

Sadly, these measures have failed to achieve the desired results, for various reasons. The principal features of the caste system – the avoidance of inter-caste competition, and the notion that contact with members of lower castes results in pollution – are on the wane, to be replaced by intense inter-caste competition for political and administrative patronage. Today, caste is increasingly seen in terms of solidarity groups. Socially, the caste hierarchy remains. In economic terms, the rich have got richer and the poor have failed to prosper. In politics, however, active players have emerged from lower-caste categories – but these beneficiaries of reform have failed to meet the aspirations of their people. Political self-interest, corruption, and nepotism have deprived others of similar opportunities.

From the national level down to the village level, the nexus between caste and politics assumes great importance. Those who seek to obtain and hold on to political power often look to particular *jatis* as potential 'vote banks'. Alliances among caste groups, however, are subject to frequent shifts, based on short-term political expediency.

◀ Members of an adivasi (tribal) community in Tonur village, Tamil Nadu

CASTES AND *JATI*

In South Asia the caste system has been a dominating aspect of social organisation for thousands of years. A caste, generally referred to as *jati* (birth), is a strictly regulated social community, which one is born into. A person is expected to marry within this *jati* and observe appropriate rules governing occupation, kinship, and diet. Interactions with other *jatis* are determined by the position of one's own group in the social hierarchy.

In India, virtually all non-tribal Hindus and many adherents of other faiths (even Muslims, for whom caste is theoretically anathema) recognise their membership of one of these hereditary social communities. Among Hindus, *jatis* are usually assigned to one of four large caste clusters, called *varnas*, each of which has a traditional social function. The particular *varna* in which a *jati* is ranked depends in part on its relative level of 'impurity', determined by the group's traditional contact with any of a number of 'pollutants'. Restrictions were traditionally established to protect the relative 'purity' of a particular *jati* from corruption by the 'pollution' of a lower caste.

A fifth group, the *panchamas* (from Sanskrit *panch*, 'five'), were theoretically excluded from the system because their occupations and ways of life typically brought them into contact with such impurities. Formerly called the Untouchables (because contact with them, believed to transmit pollution, was avoided), they are now designated as *harijans* ('Children of God', a term popularised by Mahatma Gandhi) and, officially, as scheduled castes. Those in scheduled castes, collectively accounting for nearly one-sixth of India's total population, are generally landless and perform most of the agricultural labour, as well as a number of ritually polluting caste-related occupations (such as leatherwork, performed by the *chamars*, who are the largest scheduled caste).

Although inherently non-egalitarian, *jatis* provide Indians with social support and, at least in theory, a sense of having a secure and well-defined social and economical role. In most parts of India, one or more dominant castes own the majority of land, exercise the greatest political power, and set a cultural tone for a particular region. A dominant *jati* typically comprises between one-eighth and one-third of the total rural population, but it may in some areas account for a clear majority. The second most numerous *jati* is usually from one of the scheduled castes. Depending on its size, a village typically will have between five and 25 *jatis*, each of which might be represented by households numbering anything from one to more than 100.

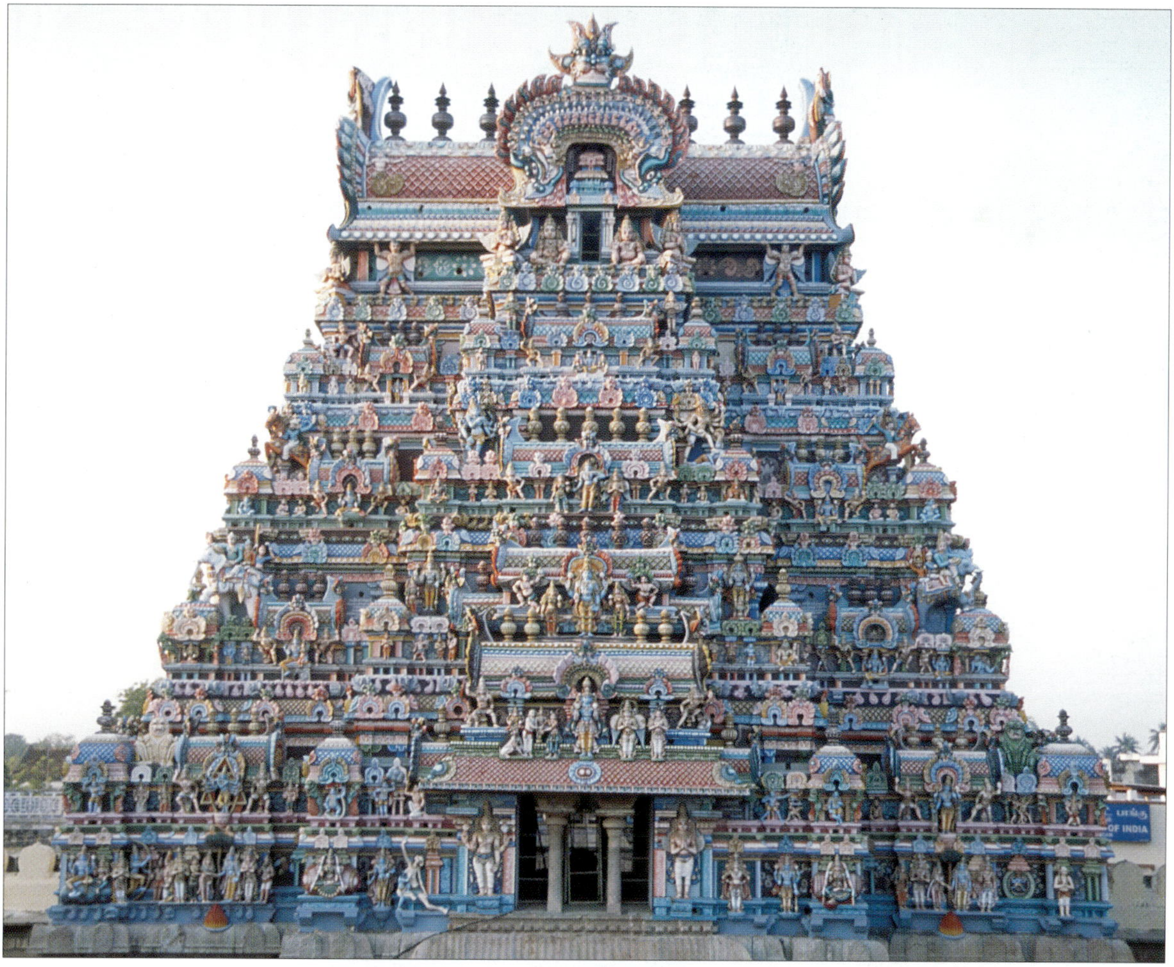

Shailan Parker/Oxfam

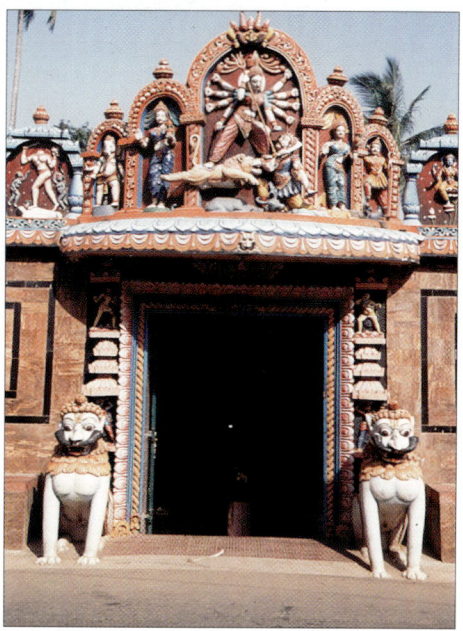

▲ *Hindu architecture, a riot of human and divine forms: Sriranganathsvami Temple, Tiruchchirappalli, Tamil Nadu.*

◄ *Classic Islamic architecture, devoid of human forms: the Golden Fort of Jaisalmer, built between 1500 and 1700 in the Thar desert, Rajasthan.*

► *The Konark Sun Temple, Orissa*

Shailan Parker/Oxfam

Shailan Parker/Oxfam

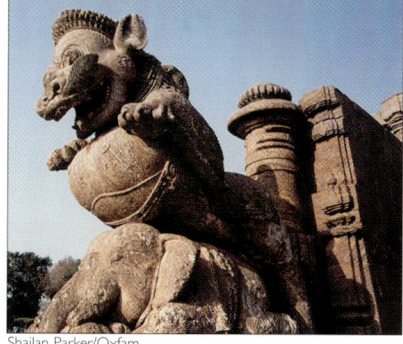

Celebrating cultural diversity

The most powerfully defining feature of Indian society is what Jawaharlal Nehru called 'the continuity of a cultural tradition through five thousand years of history'. On the Indian sub-continent, multiple cultures have co-existed in harmony for ages, except when political leaders have exploited this diversity and used it to divide people along religious and communal lines.

In independent India, official lack of understanding of ethnic aspirations has led to insurgencies and the rise of separatist movements, especially in the north-east. But the nation's democratic institutions have responded successfully to such problems. The creation of 'linguistic states' was one such response, when many state boundaries were drawn on linguistic lines. Language is a heavily politicised issue. Many efforts have been made to promote Hindi as the national language and gradually phase out English. However, although Hindi is the predominant language in the north, it bears little relation to the languages of the south, where very few speak it. English continues to be spoken by the educated, and proficiency in English is regarded as a badge of membership of the elite.

In recent times, greater ease of movement across the country, indigenous tourism, improved communications, and increased opportunity and access to resources have all played their part in promoting national integration.

Artistic heritage

In traditional Indian society there was no sharp distinction between 'art' and 'craft'. The Sanskrit word *shilpa* has been used to mean skill, craft, work of art or architecture, design, or decoration. Traditional art forms include pottery, jewellery, carpet weaving, embroidery, painting, woodwork, leatherwork, and metalwork. Craft skills and traditions, an inseparable element of the rituals and festivals of everyday life, have survived until the present day without any other form of patronage. Architecture is perhaps India's greatest triumph, as evident in Ajanta Ellora, a large relief hewn from rocks; the Sun Temple of Konark, built like a chariot in the thirteenth century; the graceful erotic sculptures of the eleventh-century temples of Khajuraho; and such Mughal masterpieces as Humayun's tomb in Delhi, and the best-known memorial of love: the Taj Mahal, built between 1630 and 1648.

Under British rule much of this creative cultural energy became dissipated, but at the same time certain individuals, such as William Carey (1761–1834) and Max Muller (1823–1900), became interested in ancient and medieval Indian culture; through their translations and commentaries, they provided Western readers with access to key works.

Performing arts, all based on music, also have a long and distinguished tradition. Dance and theatre in their classical forms are not capable of expression without music. All these art forms are a mode of religious expression, as well as an essential accompaniment to many social

▲ *Music is an essential accompaniment to many festivities in India.*

festivities, including the narration of bardic stories and folk tales. A revival of interest in aspects of Indian thought and culture accompanied the rising nationalist feeling, and the twentieth century saw efforts to revive dying arts such as *kathakali* (a highly stylised dance form of Kerala in South India), and to reconstitute early forms of traditional performing arts. Today, India is known for many internationally acclaimed artists, including the renowned *sitar* player, Ravi Shankar.

There has also been a revival of theatre. Bengali playwrights, especially Nobel Prize winner Rabindra Nath Tagore (1861–1941), have given new life to Indian theatre. However, the Indian motion-picture industry has taken the place of theatre and now constitutes not only the most popular form of mass entertainment but often a mirror of contemporary India.

In the world of letters, India counts epics written in the second century BC as its heritage, but continues to contribute to world literature through the works of modern authors such as R.K. Narayan, Salman Rushdie, Vikram Seth, and Arundhati Roy. Arundhati Roy's recent success is phenomenal. In the UK she was awarded the Booker Prize for her first novel, *God of Small Things*, in 1997; it was translated into 40 languages and sold six million copies. She has identified herself with social issues such as the anti-nuclear movement and the grassroots organisation against the Narmada Dam, the Narmada Bachao Andolan (NBA), and she voices her opposition in her prolific output of political essays.

▲ Bhiansar village, Rajasthan: Jaiti Bhai makes papier maché bowls. 'You take clay, jute, paper, grain husks, and water, and grind them all together into a paste, which you smooth over a mould. When the bowl is dry, you decorate it; I bought this pink colour, but I use green and red sometimes too.'

▲ Boys playing cricket (a national obsession in India) on the Marina Beach in Chennai

A question of numbers

Despite India's vast landmass, approximately two-thirds of all Indians live in coastal regions and in the broad Gangetic Plain. In these areas, average population density is 550–650 people per square kilometre, while the national average is 324.

In 1951, at the time of the first census, the population of independent India was 361 million. Since then it has tripled to 1027 million (2001 Census). The average annual growth rate during the ten years before Independence was only 1.25 per cent. The current figure is around 2 per cent per annum. India adds more people to the world's population each year than China does; or, to put it another way, every year the population of India increases by a figure equivalent to the entire population of Australia: approximately 20 million people.

India's rate of population growth is due more to a decline in mortality rates than to a big increase in fertility. The crude death rate has shown a steady decline: from 43 deaths per 1000 in 1901 to nine in 1994. By contrast, the decline in the crude birth rate has been slower: from 49 live births

▶ Children throng a school playground in Hyderabad. But across the country 30 million children are not in school. India spends only one per cent of its national income on primary education.

per 1000 in 1901 to 29 in 1994. While the Total Fertility Rate (TFR), or the average number of children per woman, has declined steadily from 5.97 in 1961 to 2.85 in 1999, the increase in life expectancy has been more dramatic. Between 1900 and Independence in 1947, life expectancy grew by only 10 years, but in the next five decades it grew by 30 years to 64 for males and 65 for females.

The Infant Mortality Rate (IMR) has improved through the use of immunisation programmes and oral rehydration treatment for diarrhoea; but although these measures have prevented deaths, they have not necessarily improved the quality of infants' lives. IMR has declined markedly over the last 50 years, but 25 per cent of the world's infant deaths (72 per 1000) and 20 per cent of all cases of maternal mortality (437 per 100,000) continue to take place in India.

The reduction in the birth rate was achieved through the medical intervention of manipulating fertility, rather than through social change. Since the national family-planning programme was adopted in 1950, the allocation of resources to it in each Five Year Plan has been steadily increasing. Expenditure on family planning became entrenched in programmes that were top–down, incentive-based, target-oriented, and sterilisation-focused. It was during the state of emergency in 1975–77 that 8.26 million men – a record number – were coerced into having vasectomy operations. People reacted strongly against this policy, which was one of the factors that brought down the government. The newly elected government changed the policy to 'family welfare', with emphasis on information, education, and voluntary participation.

Development is the best contraceptive

The 1994 International Conference on Population and Development (ICPD) brought about a major shift in thinking on the subject: from an emphasis on population control to a focus on individual well-being. India was a party to this new approach, and subsequently its National Population Policy of 2000 (NPP 2000) acknowledged that stabilising the population depends on giving people access to resources and information. Complex links between population, poverty, economic growth, education, and people's overall health and well-being are now increasingly seen as important elements of campaigns to stabilise the size of the population.

However, the NPP 2000 is riddled with contradictions. On the one hand, it calls for a target-free, comprehensive approach, but on the other hand it unrealistically projects replacement-level fertility rates by 2010, and a stable population by 2045. Investment in critical sectors that affect population growth, such as education services, has not so far benefited the poorest communities. Nor is there a recognition of the fact that, while reducing the population growth rate may be a desirable national goal, it is not easy to influence behaviour in groups where family size is affected by cultural norms. Nor is it sufficiently acknowledged that the typical Indian woman does not make decisions about her own fertility: her husband, his family, the community, and the State decide the number and sex of her children.

A striking revelation of the Census 2001 is that in the previous ten years there was a sharp decline in the sex ratio in the 0–6 age group: from 945 girls per 1000 boys to 927 girls per 1000 boys. What is further intriguing is that the fall is greater in economically developed states like Punjab (-82) and Haryana (-52). This suggests that economic development does not necessarily translate into greater security for women.

Another inconsistency arises when we try to identify the conditions for the decline in fertility. According to Census 2001, nine states have achieved replacement-level growth rates; but while one of them, Kerala, has a high level of female literacy (88 per cent) and low levels of infant and maternal mortality, Tamil Nadu's sharp decline in fertility has occurred without the benefit of these positive developments. In Gujarat, fertility has declined almost by 50 per cent, but IMR continues to be high, and female literacy rates are much lower than in Tamil Nadu.

It was at the 1974 World Population Conference at Bucharest that the Indian delegation coined the slogan: *Development is the best contraceptive*. More recently the proposed catchphrase is *Contraception is the best development*. In India, both these approaches are valid. Given the many contradictory facts, it is difficult to specify the threshold levels of social and economic progress that would usher in significant fertility decline and population stability.

The population profile

India's population is relatively young. This means that there is an inherent momentum for growth, which in turn is a result of high fertility in the past. There are some important implications of this trend: first, the population will continue to grow for another 50 years, until today's children have completed their prime reproductive phase. Secondly, the absolute number of children needing education will continue to grow for some time. Thirdly, the rapid growth of the economically active population will require a steady increase in jobs.

The proportion of old people has remained almost static over the past few decades, but has increased in absolute terms. So over the next 30–40 years more resources will have to be allocated to meet the needs of the elderly.

▼ *Old man, Rajasthan*

30 INDIA

▲ *Kolkata: a morning wash at a broken water-main for a family of street-dwellers*

Migrating to urban jungles

In India the trend towards urbanisation began when refugees from partition moved into towns and cities. Makeshift refugee colonies and shanty settlements proliferated. By 1951 the population of Delhi had doubled to 1.4 million, and those of Kolkata, Mumbai (formerly known as Bombay), Chennai (formerly Madras), and Hyderabad had exceeded one million each. The National Institute of Urban Affairs estimates that if the present rate of urbanisation continues, by the year 2021 half of India's population will be living in towns and cities. The signs are all there in the 2001 census: more than 285 million Indians live in urban areas; Mumbai, Kolkata, and Delhi each now support a population of more than 10 million. Much of this growth has been unplanned; the result is the creation of urban slums and ever-greater demands on municipal resources.

In recent times, a good deal of India's urbanisation process can be attributed to the disproportionate concentration of economic activity in towns and cities. People are pushed out of the countryside to cities by the lack of economic opportunities. This trend intensifies during floods, droughts, cyclones, and communal conflict; but the major contributing factors are the extension of municipal boundaries to absorb villages (killing off agricultural livelihoods and creating poverty and slums), and the natural growth of existing populations. The infrastructure in most large cities cannot cope, and municipal services are severely overburdened. Moreover, urban economic growth and job creation have not kept pace with the population explosion. This has led to a deepening of urban poverty, deprivation, and crime.

It is not entirely true to say that new jobs are not being created. Currently urban India has captured 15 per cent of the global market in information-technology services (customer care and data management) provided to the more developed economies. But this achievement has benefited only the educated and skilled – and only in the more developed states of Maharashtra, Karnataka, and Andhra Pradesh. The degree to which economic development is unbalanced in India can be assessed from the fact that 40 per cent of all overseas phone calls are made to and from Mumbai, in western India.

The capital, Delhi, has 1,400,000 homeless people and four million slum dwellers, lacking most basic services such as safe drinking water and sanitation. But some elected representatives encourage the formation of slums and are reluctant to relocate them, for fear of losing a significant element of political support. On-site development schemes, providing housing with rights of tenure, are not always feasible, because they encourage encroachment on public land.

Slums, squatter colonies, and resettlement localities are a reality in every metropolis, and so is the disparity in access to resources such as education, housing, water, and sewage disposal. Even in cities claiming to supply water to every sector of the community, rich households consume ten times more than poor ones. For instance, in Ahmedabad 25 per cent of the population consumes 90 per cent of the water. In Kolkata, slum areas receive 20 gallons per person per day, while non-slum areas are supplied with 60 gallons per person per day.

Indore: slum dwellers assert the right to decent housing

In Indore, the commercial capital of Madhya Pradesh (MP), approximately 45 per cent of the city population lives in slums, but the areas in question occupy only 8 per cent of the total residential space in the city. A few kilometres from the bright, kitschy city centre, in the slums adjoining Surya Dev Nagar, lives Asha Wag, one of the million poor people in a city of 1.6 million. Her many skills include bangle making, midwifery, and home making, but it is for her leadership qualities that her community respects her.

When her former home in Bhagat Singh Nagar was pulled down to accommodate a city-beautification scheme, Asha and her household moved to Surya Dev Nagar, along with 198 other families. The relocation process began in 1995. Although her community had the status of permanent residence in Bhagat Singh Nagar, having been allotted rights of tenure by the government in recognition of the duration of their occupation, even so they were told that they would be evicted. Crucial questions were left unanswered: *Where will we go, and how will we get there? How are we to earn a living? What about our legal rights?*

Squalor and insecurity blight the lives of millions of urban slum dwellers in India. But the difference in this case was that MP and Rajasthan are the two states that acknowledge the needs of the urban poor in their policy on the allocation of residential land. In 1982 the MP government

▲ Mrs Asha Wagh: 'We demanded the right to stay here.'

Women in the slums of Indore can earn £4–6 each month by making bangles.

announced that an area of 5 per cent in all residential projects must be reserved for the poor. In 1987 this figure was increased to 15 per cent. In practice, however, little land has been reserved, for reasons that inevitably include bureaucratic delays: for example, the policy permits land to revert to the developer if not allocated to beneficiaries within two years.

Unknown to Asha, *Deen Bandhu Samajik Sanstha* (DBSS) had been monitoring the resettlement plans of the city government. This non-government organisation has campaigned for housing rights for poor urban communities since 1994; it also organises them to demand their legal and constitutional entitlements. DBSS has successfully acquired 228 acres of land in the city and prevented slum dwellers like Asha from being relocated to areas where there are no basic amenities, public transport, or opportunities for earning a livelihood.

'Initially Rajeev George of DBSS contacted us, the women, to organise ourselves into informal savings and loan groups. Our capital soon grew, and we decided to invest in bangle making. This activity is very popular now, since each of us can make £4–£6 per month: enough to educate three children. Having brought us together, he helped us to tackle other issues, such as claiming our rights and benefits under various government schemes – widows' pensions, ration cards, credit for small businesses, and inclusion in the voters' list. But the chief issue for us was the threat of eviction from our homes. We refused to move to the location identified by the authorities. We demanded the right to stay in this area, which was not only the most suitable but also rightfully ours, since it had been assigned to the poor – if only on paper. Perhaps for the first time in the history of Indore, the government gave in to the demands of poor people', says Asha proudly.

DBSS has conducted a slum-mapping exercise, to produce an information base that ordinary people can consult. It contains valuable details about land use in the city, as specified in the Indore Master Plan of 1974. Slum dwellers themselves have accumulated information about the location of homes, the resources available, and the provision of facilities like drains, electricity, and roads. Asha's community has been quoting from the Master Plan, which was designed to safeguard the interests of all sections of society but over the years has been violated to the extent that basic amenities and services have collapsed.

Responding to lobbying by DBSS, the local government has begun the process of identifying appropriate alternative sites before evicting slum dwellers. Poor communities have formed a 'Slum Forum', through which they will assert their rights and claim their entitlements. The members are not only taking part in advocacy at the city and state levels but also engaging with the newly formed National Forum for Housing Rights (NFHR). Asha Wag and her community are now part of a global campaign against forced evictions, claiming comprehensive housing provision for all inhabitants.

'Sadly,' says Rajeev George, 'it is not eviction from squalid conditions that violates the right to decent housing, but the conditions that force people to settle in them in the first place.'

Economy and trade

▲ *Kolkata: a street hawker selling magazines. India has no shortage of entrepreneurs.*

At the time of Independence, India inherited an economy that was mainly geared to supplying the demands of the imperial power. The new nation was poor, with a predominantly agrarian economy and a negligible industrial base. However, it possessed a potentially large domestic market, rich natural resources, considerable supplies of skilled and semi-skilled labour, no shortage of entrepreneurs, and a political leadership that was seemingly committed to development.

By the mid-1950s India had abandoned the colonial free-market policy of *laissez faire*. Inspired by the socialist convictions of Prime Minister Nehru, it established the state-directed planning process that would define its development pattern for the next 40 years. The prime objectives were to achieve sound industrial development, economic independence, and the political survival of the nation. Rapid industrialisation was expected to provide the impetus to achieve growth and prosperity. To increase its self-reliance, India set out to manufacture products that previously it had imported, discouraging imports by an extensive system of licensing and high tariffs. There was a crucial role for central planning and the public sector, and an emphasis on heavy industry.

By the late 1970s, however, it was becoming obvious that Indian economic and trade policies were not achieving their objectives. The government responded by giving larger scope to the private sector and modifying its trade policies. The immediate results were encouraging, but not sustained; government expenditure increased rapidly, while investment slowed down. Export subsidies, food subsidies, fertiliser subsidies, power subsidies – all part of the government's policy to encourage new technology in farming – increased the financial burden on the nation.

By 1991, foreign-exchange reserves had dwindled to little more than US $1 billion, barely sufficient to finance ten days' normal import needs. So the process of opening up the Indian economy to foreign trade and investment began. Since the reforms initiated in 1991, the economic health of the nation might be expressed as 'getting better, and feeling worse'.

During the 1990s, India's gross domestic product (GDP) grew at a rate of more than 5 per cent. The bad news, however, is that national debts have increased. As of 31 March 2001, India's external debts stood at approximately $ 100 billion, which meant that every Indian man, woman, and child owed $100 to the rest of the world. The extent of internal debt is alarming. General government debt rose from 67 per cent of GDP at the end of March 1997 to 88 per cent of GDP by the end of March 2003. Per capita income remains one of the lowest in the world: more than a quarter of the population lives below the official poverty line and, despite an agricultural revolution and overflowing granaries, deaths from starvation have continued (for example, in West Orissa in 2001–2002). For millions of people a secure supply of food is an impossibility. A large proportion of India's population has no access to safe drinking water or primary health-care services.

Strengths and weaknesses of the Indian economy

▼ *A power station on the outskirts of Ahmedabad*

The Indian economy today presents a mixed picture of great potential strengths and significant vulnerabilities. On the positive side, India is globally recognised as a leader in the provision of some important manufacturing and technology-based services. Domestic savings and investment rates have been fairly high for several years. Power, transport, and other infrastructural sectors, although inadequate, are being strengthened to support rapid economic growth. Key services like banking, insurance, telecommunications, and electronic media are being rapidly modernised, and the country has a large pool of entrepreneurs, managers, scientists, technologists, and other highly skilled professional people.

Shailan Parker/Oxfam

▲ *Everything on Bhutni Island in the Phulahar river, West Bengal, has to be brought from the mainland by boat. India needs major investment to improve national transport and communications networks.*

Yet in spite of these developments, India is still blighted by poverty, illiteracy, malnutrition, and all manner of material deprivation on a vast scale. With a still-rising population, life in India's villages is becoming harsher for the poor, whose access to land, food, fuel, and other basic essentials is diminishing, rather than increasing. The pace of urbanisation has quickened, and India's cities and towns are grudging hosts to a large and rising class of urban poor who have no shelter, drinking water, sanitation, health care, or remunerative employment.

It is ironic that on the one hand India can build atomic power stations, make nuclear weapons, and launch satellites into space, yet is unable to provide safe drinking water or sanitation for its citizens. Modern and primitive conditions prevail in close proximity. Liberal humanitarian and democratic value systems contend with superstitious, obscurantist, and atavistic attitudes. The process of modernisation itself has probably sharpened this contrast and has added to the potential for conflict in society.

The paradox of poverty-alleviation programmes

The persistence of poverty in independent India has been a subject of extensive research and intensive debate. Yet neither government spending on poverty-alleviation programmes nor sustained economic growth, averaging 5–6 per cent in the past 20 years, has made any major difference to the long-term prospects for the poorest, or even met their basic minimum needs.

India's various Five-Year Plans have contained commitments to economic and social change in order to reduce inequalities of income, wealth, and opportunity, especially in the rural areas. But peasant farmers and wage workers alike have been affected by the government's structural adjustment policies, which have resulted in a rise in the prices of commodities, especially food; a drop in real wages; and a loss of jobs as public services and enterprises have been privatised.

In theory, the government still subsidises essential supplies of food and fuel for the poorest people. The annual bill is very considerable. If the money were to be given directly as cash transfers to the 26 per cent of the population that lives below the poverty line, each poor household would get around Rs 8000 (approximately £95) a year. But out of every rupee that is spent on food subsidies, only 20 per cent actually reaches the poor. This is well documented in the case of the PDS (Public Distribution System), which – because it is not targeted or implemented properly – mostly benefits people who live above the poverty line. Any attempt at reform is challenged by strong vested interests.

Power supplies are another example of hijacked subsidies. A subsidy that was intended to help poor farmers to run equipment like irrigation pumps and threshing machines has been appropriated by industry. It is difficult to persuade this rich sector of the economy to pay for something that it has been in the habit of obtaining for free.

In the post-reform period, poverty has declined at very varying rates. The state of Haryana, for example, has managed to reduce the proportion of its people living in absolute poverty from 25 per cent to 9 per cent; but in Orissa the corresponding figure has merely been reduced from 49 to 47 per cent. This disappointing performance can be explained by a host of factors: low levels of skills, education, and health care; inadequate infrastructure; a hostile economic-policy environment; and, most significantly, the poor quality of governance. But it is also true that the lack of money – the obvious definition of poverty – makes people more vulnerable to every adverse influence on their lives.

Signs of hope

On 26 January 2001, the village of Hangia Vand was devastated in the earthquake that struck Gujarat. The families of 52-year-old Rambhai Pancha Bhai and 22-year-old Bhachu Mansangh, largely dependent on daily wage labour, were reduced to destitution. But their community unanimously nominated them as beneficiaries of the relief and development aid that arrived in the village.

▼ *The camel cart given to Bhachu Mansangh after the earthquake in Gujarat*

Shailan Parker/Oxfam

'Our lives were transformed', says Rambhai Pancha Bhai. 'Until then we did not have electricity, since no one had the money to install meters, and the elders said that it was too dangerous. Now there is electricity. Concrete dwellings have replaced our thatched roofs. Our main requirement was a secure livelihood. What would we eat, and how would we earn our living? The villagers asked Oxfam for help, and the community selected the beneficiaries and decided that we needed a flour-mill here. I now own a mill, and Bhachu was given a camel cart,

▲ *A flood-preparedness course in West Bengal: volunteers learn to make a raft using local materials — empty oil cans, bamboo, and rope.*

on which he loads goods for sale in towns nearby. The village community does not allow any shops here, because they always stock *gutka* [tobacco] and *beedi* [unprocessed rolled tobacco], with easy access for children.'

Hangia Vand village is in the sparsely populated Kutch region, which was the epicentre of the earthquake. The disaster was devastating for everyone, but even more so for already impoverished people like Rambhai Pancha Bhai and Bhachu Mansangh. While they have benefited from post-disaster support programmes by acquiring long-term skills and tools with which to earn a living, there are many who continue to suffer from recurring disasters, both sudden (earthquakes) and regular (cyclones, floods, and droughts).

Dealing with disasters – in advance

Cyclones threaten Ishanapur, Jajpur District of coastal Orissa, almost every year, with varying degrees of intensity. In the month of April, Babaji Barik has approximately two months before the cyclone season in which to replace his hut with a concrete structure. 'We are re-learning things that used to be standard procedure in olden times. We had rice strains that were resistant to water logging, but they are not easily available any more. We used to keep our livestock untethered, so that they could instinctively flee to safety. And we even had traditional methods of forecasting cyclones. What is better now is the commitment of organisations like *Lok Bikash* to help us to help ourselves. They introduced us to the community-action approach to preparing for disasters and responding to them: methods of ensuring clean drinking water, preventing epidemics, and taking advantage of government schemes and information. In fact I am building this place with the support that I received through the *Indira Awas Yojana* [a government shelter which provides building materials for poor people in rural areas]. These disasters reduce everyone to poverty. I am a barber. How do I ensure my livelihood without the tools of my trade – a barber's chair, razors, blades, balms, and mirrors?'

In order to promote public awareness of the need to make plans to deal with disasters, the government of Orissa declared 29 October, the anniversary of the day on which the super cyclone struck the state in 1999, as Disaster Preparedness Day. The central government also resolved to observe this day throughout the country; but the concept of a rational disaster-management policy has yet to gain acceptance at the national level.

There is a growing realisation that institutional initiatives and people's actions have to be co-ordinated to soften the impact of disasters. The official response to calamities is often insensitive to local conditions, for example in Gujarat and Orissa, where people needed support to rebuild their livelihoods, but what was on offer was palliative at best.

▲ *Rampada Pramanik, a volunteer on a flood-response programme on Bhutni Island. 'We are on alert 24 hours a day. Five of us share out the work. Between us we look after 300 people.'*

Market access in practice: the weavers of Chacha village

In the village of Chacha, in arid Rajasthan, weaving was the traditional method of coping with drought, when all farming activity had to stop. But over centuries, as the rural poor lost their land to the upper castes, weaving became their only means of livelihood, and it gave them their caste identity.

Revata Ram, who now lives and works in Phalodi, says, 'Back in the 1960s, when I was a young boy, *meghwal* [weaver-caste] families used to produce cloth for local needs, and it was often paid for in kind. No one thought of education for the lower castes; but my uncle had studied up to the fourth grade, so, following his example, my brother and I were both enrolled in school. We sat at a distance from others, because we were low caste. We were scared to touch or speak to anyone. I went on to study until the eighth grade, when my family withdrew me from school because they couldn't afford the fees at a time of extreme drought.

'I slowly started getting involved with weaving. I realised that we could buy cheaper and more varied types of thread from Jodhpur. Soon I started stitching and providing finished products. I gained a reputation as a steady weaver, capable of producing new designs. In 1986 URMUL [*Uttari Rajasthan Milk Union Limited*] invited me to join them, because they wanted to work among the *meghwals*. My family was apprehensive, but after much hesitation I went to Lunkaransar and for the first time learned about responding to markets, about up-dating our craft by adopting contemporary designs. I got training in design from graduates of the National Institute of Design, learned chemical dyeing in Benaras, and was taught to do market surveys, stock taking, and accounting.

▼ *Revata Ram: 'I was a middle-school drop-out. Now I operate computers.'*

'Then I came back and refined the skills of weavers here. Later, along with a few others, I set up *Urmul Marusthali Bunkar Vikas Samiti* (UMBVS), a weavers' co-operative. That was in 1986. From being a middle-school drop-out, I now operate computers. My children seem to live in a different world: one is an aspiring lawyer,

▲ Hava Kadela winding thread on to a bobbin. 'A teacher in UMBVS taught me the skill of weaving. I used to earn between 25 and 30 rupees a day, doing building work. Now I work at home, and whenever I wish to. I don't have to depend on others, and I have more time with my family.'

and my daughter is in high school – something unimaginable in this region and in my community even a few years ago.'

The search for ways of using the yarn spun by women in a relief programme during the severe drought of 1985 led URMUL to work with the traditional weavers of Phalodi and Pokhran. The urge to do more than make a sustainable living – to extend benefits to the whole *meghwal* community – became the foundation for the UMBVS. Generations of oppression had left the weavers socially and economically weak, but the UMBVS not only secured the livelihoods of 170 families but also increased their self-esteem. At present, about 15 per cent of the weavers are women. 'We intend to increase their participation to at least 40 per cent,' says Revata Ram, 'but it is a slow process, because weaving is not traditionally women's work.'

Traditional designs, colours, and products, combined with constant exposure and response to customer preferences, have resulted in a wider range of products. For the *meghwal* weavers, gone are the days when they had to carry their shoes in their hands while passing the houses of the powerful. Marketing and sourcing orders in Delhi, Mumbai, and Kolkata are the new challenges. Fifty per cent of production in the recent past was for foreign markets, as diverse as New Zealand and Japan. 'Export marketing is difficult, because it is time-bound and quantities are huge. But we have regular clients. In the last financial year our turnover was approximately £556,800', volunteers Revata Ram with pride.

The UMBVS experience demonstrates that change is possible, although secure market-access opportunities are essential for sustainable development.

Indian textiles on the world market

India has been a centre for cotton weaving for many centuries. Indian textiles, produced on handlooms as far back as two thousand years ago, were prized for their fineness of weave, brilliance of colour, and rich variety of design. Today, the textile and clothing industry contributes around 14 per cent of India's total industrial production, and 37 per cent of its exports. It is the second largest employer in the country, after agriculture. But India accounts for only 3 per cent of world trade in textiles and clothing, partly because it has not enjoyed better access to the markets of industrial countries. Since 1974, India's textile and clothing trade has been governed by the restrictive quota regime imposed by the Multi-Fibre Arrangement (MFA), a protectionist measure which restrains the growth of textile and clothing exports from developing countries.

During the Uruguay Round of world trade talks, industrialised countries agreed to dismantle the MFA in four stages over a ten-year period, starting in 1995. The expected benefits, however, have been slow to materialise, because the phase-out was delayed until the very end of 2004. Compounding the problem are other restrictive measures taken by importing countries, such as 'transitional safeguards' (which allow importing countries to restrict sudden large influxes of imports) and discriminatory 'rules of origin' (which allow imports to be taxed at high levels if a certain proportion of their inputs comes from another country).

With the ending of the quota system, the value of the global textile and clothing trade is expected to reach $400 billion. The Indian government wants to increase textile and garment exports from the current levels of $11 billion to $50 billion. To achieve this ambitious target, the industry needs to become more competitive, its infrastructure and technology must be modernised, and it must stop being sheltered by protectionist, inward-looking policies. But will Revata Ram and UMBVS have the skills and resources that they need in order to reach wider markets?

India and the WTO

India joined the World Trade Organisation in 1995 as a founder member. Membership of the WTO confers advantages and disadvantages. With a share in international trade that amounts to a mere 0.7 per cent, it would be over-optimistic of India to hope to influence the rules of the game in a big way. But it takes an active part in negotiations, often in coalition with other developing countries, and is effective in drawing attention to the way in which some new trade rules that are being advocated by the rich countries, ostensibly for the benefit of all, may harm the development prospects of poor countries.

India has taken a leading role in the formation and activities of the G-20, a pressure group of developing countries that has recently emerged at the WTO to promote reform of the unfair agricultural policies of the developed countries. They want the rich countries to open their markets to goods from developing countries, and they want the European Union and the United States to stop subsidising their own farmers. India also argues forcefully for developing countries to be granted a longer period of time in which to open their markets to manufactured and agricultural imports. More than any other country, it has raised concerns about excessive protection of intellectual property rights, including patents and copyrights. During the WTO conference in Doha in November 2001, India succeeded in securing a major concession on the right to manufacture cheap versions of new patented medicines. Currently, India and other developing countries oppose the introduction of labour standards and environmental standards into WTO rules, on the ground that these are disguised 'non-tariff' barriers to free and fair trade.

Globalisation of the world economy is here to stay, and market forces and the profit motive will prevail. But in this context, India is arguing that much more could be done by the richer countries to achieve equity and justice for the developing world.

▼ *The textile and garment industry is the second largest employer in India. But it needs to modernise if it is to be competitive on world markets.*

India's untapped human potential

India's potential wealth, measured in terms of human capital, is immense – but largely untapped. Despite the country's abundant assets, and particularly its rich human resources, its economic and social advancement has been slow, for reasons that will be explored in this chapter.

It was in 1985 that a separate Ministry of Human Resource Development was formed, merging the ministries of education, culture, youth, and women's development. This was a multi-dimensional, dynamic concept which aimed to make India more productive by upgrading public services. Since then, central government's expenditure on education, health, family welfare, water supply, housing, social welfare, nutrition, rural employment, and minimum basic services has been steadily increasing. By 2000, it stood at 11.4 per cent (1.7 per cent of GDP).

The statistics, however, belie the true picture, because sharp disparities continue to exist within India between states, between women and men, and between city and countryside. For example, Kerala's progress in reducing poverty is 120 times better than that of Bihar. In 2001, the Bihar literacy rate was only 47 per cent, compared with 91 per cent in Kerala. Among women too, the highest rate was in Kerala (88 per cent) and the lowest in Bihar (34 per cent).

From being one of the three richest states in 1947, Bihar has slid to the second-lowest place, with a society that is caste-ridden, poverty-stricken, and criminalised. Out of the state's total population of 100 million, half live below the poverty line. No serious efforts have been made to implement poverty-alleviation programmes, or reform education, health, and welfare schemes. With weak enforcement of law and order, coupled with lack of infrastructure, the state is not attracting investment; so the vast majority of the population can find work only as unskilled, poorly paid, manual labourers.

> One-sixth of the world's people and one-third of the world's poor live in India. India accounts for 30 per cent of the world's births, 20 per cent of the world's maternal deaths, and 25 per cent of the world's child deaths. More than half of India's children are malnourished. Two-thirds of city dwellers lack sanitation services, and one-third lack safe drinking water. About four million Indians are infected with HIV, and more than two million develop active tuberculosis every year. Only 54 per cent of women are literate, compared with 76 per cent of males.

Bridging the literacy gap

In Ramdev Peer Vand village in Gujarat, 17-year-old Ramila makes a pretty picture as she sits embroidering in the doorway. She is also watching over her 9-year-old twin brothers, who play close by in their school uniforms. 'My brothers used to go to school. Their school was run very efficiently by some *sanstha* [NGO] until it was destroyed by the earthquake in January 2001. The school has since been rebuilt and taken over by the government. Now there is no teacher, but a fancy new school building. All children were given uniforms, so they just wear them and play around the whole day. What is the point of sending them to school or even building schools?'

Ramila has not even considered the possibility of going to school herself. She is one of the 18 per cent of the population who have never enrolled. Among those who do enrol, 35 per cent drop out before completing primary-level schooling. She began to help with household chores from a very early age and, as she grew older, her burden grew disproportionately to include fetching water, collecting fuel-wood and fodder, cooking, cleaning, and caring for her brothers and sisters.

Ramdev Peer Vand village is typical of all that is wrong with India's education system. Despite the fact that nearly 95 per cent of the country's rural population lives within walking distance of a primary school, education is inaccessible for many of them, for various reasons: the poor condition of school buildings and other facilities; the shortage of teaching aids, books, and materials; and most crucially the lack of teachers. For girls, the

▶ *Girls are keen to learn, but poor provision and family responsibilities mean that nine out of ten fail to complete Grade 8.*

▼ *Ramila: 17 years old, and never been to school – like 18 per cent of the population of India*

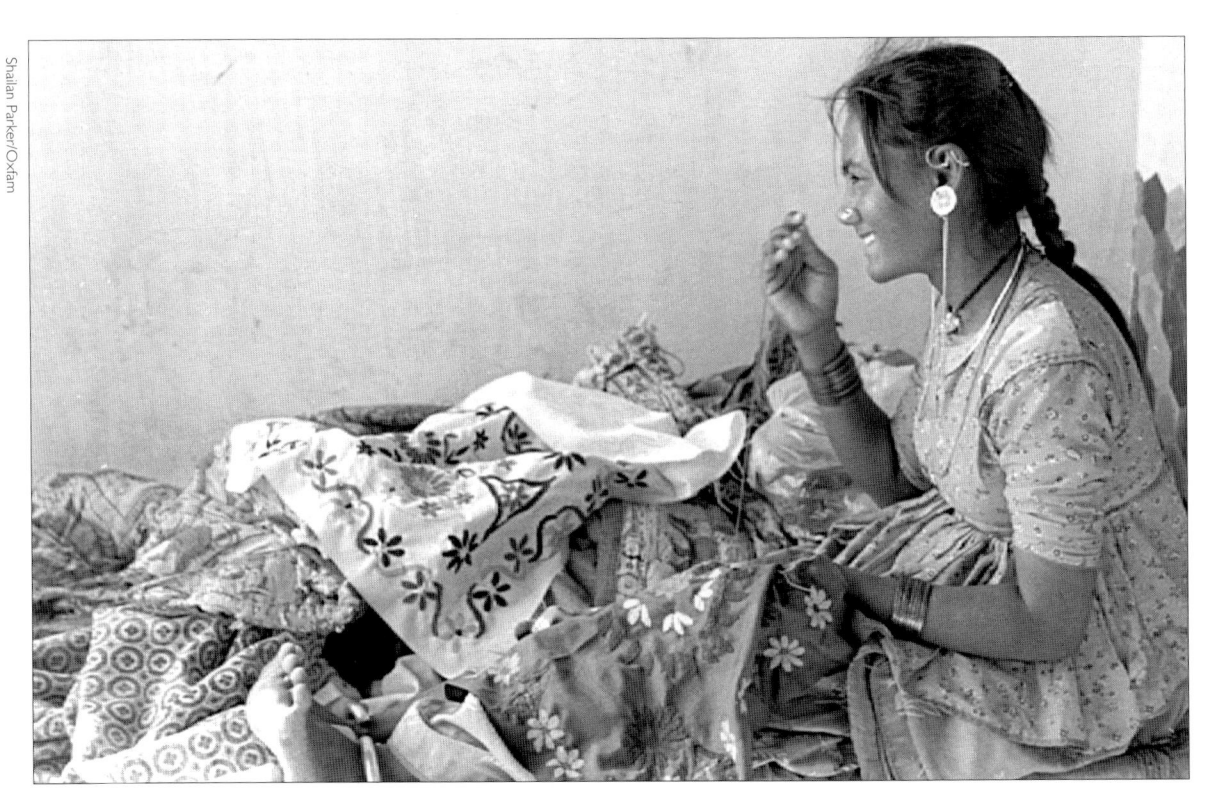

enrolment rate is even lower than for boys: economic factors, cultural conditions, and a failure to guarantee their safety once they reach adolescence play a major part in keeping girls out of school.

More than 50 years ago, the constitution of India affirmed the right of all children to free and compulsory education up to the age of 14. This milestone was to be reached within ten years of Independence: that is, by 1960. Today, the goal has shifted further into the future. India now expects to achieve universal education by 2010.

If the population continues to grow at the present rate, in order to send Ramila and others like her to school and to provide 100 per cent primary education, in the next ten years the government would need to accommodate 120 million more students in schools and enrol four million more teachers, which would require an increase in spending on education to at least 6 per cent of the GDP from the present 3.7 per cent.

GIRL POWER IN THE DESERT

In Rambagh village (Rajasthan), five 17-year-old girls courageously challenged traditional assumptions about the place of girls and women in society. Sharda, Rashmi, Sumitra, Indira, and Radha were among the first group of girls who attended the innovative *Balika Shivir*, or Girls' Camp programme, founded in Lunkaransar by URMUL (Uttari Rajasthan Milk Union Limited) in 1998.

This six-month residential programme for girls between the ages of 12 and 18 years who have never attended school has the ambitious objective of getting them admitted to the sixth standard in formal schools. The programme was established in response to the needs of girls who had had no education, after spending their childhoods in housework and caring for younger brothers and sisters.

The curriculum included anything but housework. The girls learned to read and count, to cycle and play volleyball. Hygiene and health were on the syllabus, as were conversation and public speaking. The students expanded their horizons by travelling to distant places by bus and train.

Initially, parents and elders resisted the idea. But now, five years down the line, girls who have been through the programme have become role models for others from 114 villages in the Lunkaransar district. The numbers enrolled have increased from 100 to 250. According to Ganga, one of the organisers of the camp, 'Compared with their urban counterparts, these girls have superior life skills, and their approach to learning is enthusiastic and practical.'

Out of this group of five girls, four have since married; but they refuse to leave their maternal homes until they turn 18. Sharda will not marry until she becomes a qualified teacher. The girls are supported in their decisions by an encouraging village and converted families.

The government and NGOs like URMUL are experimenting with schemes to improve attendance and retention in school. In several states, hot cooked mid-day meals have been introduced. Over ten years, *Shiksha Karmi* and *Lok Jumbis* programmes, promoting community management of schools, dramatically improved Rajasthan's literacy rate to 61 per cent in 2001 – an increase of 22 per cent, while the national average increased only by 13 per cent. Andhra Pradesh has adopted an innovative concept of community ownership of schools. Madhya Pradesh and Uttar Pradesh have decentralised management of schools to PRIs (*Panchayati Raj Institutions*). Bihar, with the lowest literacy rates in India, has launched an attendance scholarship scheme.

Despite these initiatives, the gap in literacy between girls and boys remains daunting: more than ten percentage points in all states except Kerala, Meghalaya, and Mizoram. It may be a long time before all the girls like Ramila can go to school. On the other hand, URMUL's initiative proves the demand for literacy, and contradicts assumptions about parents' reluctance to send girls to school.

How much is a mother's life worth?

Meeran has been a *dai* (traditional birth attendant), attending to women in Bhiansar, Rajasthan, ever since she can remember. Her mother-in-law initiated her into this vocation when she was 13 years old. 'A lot has changed since then – though not necessarily for the better', she rues. From earning less than one rupee per delivery, she now earns Rs 30 (approximately 35 pence). Despite increasing demand for her services, her work conditions have not improved. 'We are culturally acceptable and locally available; women trust us with their lives, but the government begrudges us even half a rupee', she complains, referring to the money allotted by the government for each '*Dai* Delivery Kit', consisting of sterilised thread, a needle, and a blade in a plastic bag. Ten years ago, the kit also contained cotton wool, but that has since been eliminated in response to the reduced purchasing power of the same 'half a rupee'.

In India, most women in rural communities give birth at home under the care of a *dai* and/or a relative or neighbour. The central role of a *dai* varies in different cultural settings: she acts as a companion to the new mother during her 20-day period of isolation among some tribes in the north-east; she serves as a wet nurse in Goa; but she is called in only to clean up after delivery in Bihar, where she is called *Dabrain* – an abusive word in the local dialect.

The typical *dai* is a low-caste, low-status woman. Such women have been marginalised by the male-dominated traditional healing professions, so they get little remuneration or social recognition in return for their services. While this huge parallel health-care system remains neglected, 300 Indian women continue to die every day of causes related to childbirth or pregnancy.

▶ Meeran (second right), a traditional birth attendant in Rajasthan, earns approximately 35 pence for each delivery that she attends.

Insufficient and inefficient health facilities have taken their toll on the health of women and children. This is evident not just in the high rates of infant and maternal mortality, but in the host of health problems that scar their lives. Malnutrition is common among children, especially girls, making them prey to almost every childhood disease. Immunisable diseases have declined dramatically as a result of a sustained immunisation programme, but they are still common among poor rural communities.

The Indian public health services have achieved some successes. In order to accelerate the eradication of polio, 'Pulse Polio Immunization' was launched in 1995–96, aiming to reach all children below the age of 3. In the next year, the target was increased to all children below the age of 5. During 1999–2000 in the four nationwide rounds more than 146 million children each time were immunised. There has been a significant decline in the number of polio cases reported. In 2002, however, 1500 cases came to light, and the immunisation campaign continues.

Up to 85 per cent of Indian women are anaemic, which increases their susceptibility to other diseases, especially during pregnancy and delivery. There is growing concern about the extent of reproductive-tract infections, cervical cancer, and sexually transmitted diseases, including HIV; but very few women seek medical care, deterred either by the absence of accessible health services, or by the social stigma associated with these diseases. Older women in India are a medically marginalised group, because women's health is perceived as being synonymous with family planning and reproductive health. Thus post-menopausal health does not figure in government health policies.

18 hospital beds for 100,000 people

India is today a major provider of health services and medical products – but not to its own people. It is the government's constitutional obligation to provide free health care to all its citizens, and over the years the infrastructure has expanded – but the focus remains on hospital-based curative services, rather than on services to prevent disease, promote good health, and rehabilitate patients. There is a danger of 'over-professionalising' health care and excluding the community as a potential resource, although recent policies have tried to involve local organisations in health care. Public funds for health are not well targeted to meet the needs of poor people, especially those living in rural areas and in the poorer regions, such as the tribal areas. India today faces a dual challenge: the burden of infectious and communicable diseases on the one hand, and an increase in chronic and lifestyle-related diseases on the other.

At 5 per cent of its GDP, India's expenditure on health care matches that of other developing countries, but it is low when measured on a per capita basis. As a consequence, India lags behind on key health indicators such as life expectancy, infant mortality, and morbidity. Less than 15 per cent of the population is formally covered through any kind of insurance, and money spent on health care comes from household income that could otherwise be spent on food, education, clothing, and shelter.

India had only 17 medical colleges in 1947. There are 180 today, producing 17,000 medical graduates and 3500 post-graduates every year. But 89 per cent of them eventually take up private practice. Sixty per cent of all hospitals are private, and more than half of these are located in urban areas. In rural areas, there are only 18 hospital beds per 100,000 people, compared with 256 in urban areas.

Government-run facilities are not generally preferred by the public, because of the callous attitudes of many medical and auxiliary staff, the shortage of drugs and other supplies, insanitary conditions, and the indifference of the government to the need for reforms. It is estimated that an additional 750,000 beds (from the current 1.5 million to 2.25 million) would be required by 2012. Apart from increasing the availability of health services, this

▼ *The poster reads 'Drink safe, arsenic-free water and stay healthy'. Arsenic poisoning affects 30 million people in the Ganges basin in West Bengal. Tube wells in many villages are affected, and now some outlying areas of Kolkata are experiencing the same problem.*

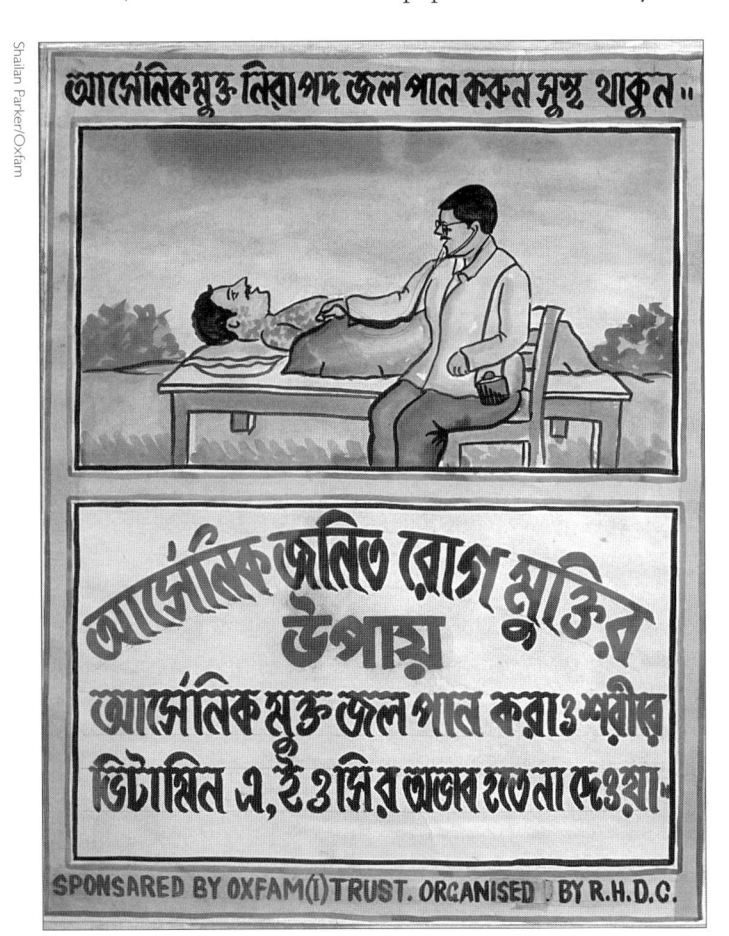

▲ Sumati Sahu: 'My mother says that girls should not suffer as her generation did, out of ignorance. Now, through our work, girls know what to expect after marriage.'

would trigger wider benefits like increased life expectancy, a reduced disease burden, and lower rates of child mortality and maternal mortality. The results would be greater national income and a richer quality of human capital.

HIV/AIDS – no longer an abstract threat

Sumati Sahu, in Bada Gobindpur, Orissa, says: 'I am a youth leader, although at 24 I am not exactly a young woman. I was attacked by a bear when I was in the forest picking *kendu* [tobacco] leaves twelve years ago. I had to drop out of school, because everyone made fun of my disfigured face. I know I will never marry, but now I don't mind. I am a counsellor and confidante of the young people here, a very satisfying responsibility.

'Last year I was inspired by the work of VYK (*Vishwa Yuva Kendra*), which raises awareness about HIV/AIDS, and I became a volunteer. Since I belong here, I am aware of the social taboos surrounding sex education. The boys and girls in the community have questions that are seldom answered. I began by meeting girls, once a month, and discussing their needs for information and the dangers that arise from lack of awareness. Cultural resistance to providing sex education to young people exposes them to trafficking, unwanted pregnancies, unsafe abortions, sexually transmitted diseases, and HIV.

'We speak to the 12–18 age group. Starting with menstrual hygiene, we impress upon girls the importance of not marrying before the age of 20. To begin with, sex education was difficult, but now I can speak more confidently – especially since the community has been so encouraging. My mother says that girls should not suffer as her generation did, out of ignorance. Now, through us, girls know what to expect after marriage, how to recognise sexually transmitted diseases, and how to prevent AIDS through the use of condoms. But my worry is that girls here are submissive. They don't become assertive, if at all, until a few years after marriage. Isn't the damage already done by then?'

Across the village in the local primary school, Sanjay, Babulal, Sandeep, and a few other boys are meeting for similar reasons. Sanjay Kumar, aged 22, says: 'Our group of 21 youths in the 15–30 age group used to meet to organise festivals and provide other services to the community. Our contact with VYK has made us realise the importance of HIV / AIDS awareness and education, especially since we know very little about our bodies. This knowledge is important, because most of us are sexually active but ignorant. Our only sources of information were textbooks and maybe grandmothers and sisters-in-law. Men don't speak to children – that is how they consider us.

▲ *Truck driver Ramesh Takri: 'I always carry condoms with me so that I don't get infections.' Because of the nature of their work – away from home for long stretches of time, travelling all over the country – truck drivers are especially at risk of HIV infection, and especially likely to spread it.*

'Ever since we became aware of the dangers of indiscriminate and irresponsible sex, we have been convinced that HIV infection rates could become immense here. When we spoke at home about this initiative, we were amazed at the support we received: we could actually talk openly about something which has always been denied until now. The community of migrant workers and drivers here respond well when we suggest that they should have regular medical checks and use condoms. This proves that everyone was keen to know but didn't know whom to ask. In fact, we provide condoms to all of them.'

Both Sumati Sahu and Sanjay Kumar are part of an HIV/AIDS intervention programme in 40 villages of Angul District in Orissa. Using peer-group discussions, it is successfully disseminating information to young people. As a result, there is a new and perceptible confidence among them to talk about sex, sexuality, and condoms.

In Orissa 17 per cent of females and 20 per cent of males are infected with sexually transmitted diseases, and there are some 2000 HIV-positive cases in the state. There are several reasons why people in Orissa are particularly vulnerable to HIV/AIDS. They include poverty; unsettled migrant communities displaced by droughts, floods, and cyclones; the highway that crosses the state, bringing drivers who can afford to buy sexual services, and who thus spread infection; and also the cultural acceptance of commercial sex work among some tribes.

In India, as in most places, current statistics are unreliable. UNAIDS estimates that four million Indians were HIV-positive in 2001; official government figures concur with that estimate. But other agencies suggest that the number could be much higher: between five and eight million.

In India HIV was first diagnosed in the mid-1980s. The urban centres were the early high-risk areas. The disease then spread through two geographic pathways: first, along the main trunk roads that serve as the transport network for this enormous country, and second, through the border regions near Burma (Myanmar), where injecting drug use is widespread. But firm conclusions are difficult to reach, since surveys are limited and people are reluctant to discuss behaviour that contributes to the spread of the disease.

The government's response to the threat of HIV/AIDS has been inconsistent. A National AIDS Control Programme was announced in 1987, but follow-through was haphazard, and the government's own anti-AIDS organisation devoted much of its energies to arguing that external groups were overestimating the prevalence of HIV in India. The National AIDS Control Organisation (NACO) has a policy of 'targeted interventions', largely based on campaigns to change people's sexual behaviour. In the last few years, NGOs have combined to offer care, support, and treatment to affected people, and to lobby the government for laws on HIV and for better prevention strategies. More recently, the government has responded to the growing demand from NGOs and community groups for anti-retroviral medication to be supplied free of charge to people affected with HIV/AIDS in six high-risk states.

India is currently in the second phase of a ten-year government programme to combat the spread of HIV. The country's federal system, however, grants wide latitude to individual states, which have shown varying levels of interest and competence in dealing with the problem. In April 2002, New Delhi announced a nationwide target of 'zero new infections by 2007'. But how is this to be achieved? Since then HIV prevalence has increased overall by 15 per cent.

▼ *A worker with the Chennai-based People's Action Movement shows members of a women's group how to use condoms.*

Out of the shadows: the place of women in Indian society

Sita and Draupadi are the two dominant female figures in Indian mythology. Sita was the consort of Prince Rama in the ancient Hindu epic called *Ramayana*, in which she symbolises purity and unconditional devotion to the husband. Draupadi, the consort of five brothers in the *Mahabharata* (an epic containing the *Gita* – guiding principles of Indian religious life), symbolises the aggressive assertion of selfhood. Ironically, both figures are deified. But the fact is that Indian women have been oppressed and subjugated for centuries.

The life of the average Indian woman is one of discrimination and deprivation in every sphere. As a child she is fed less nutritious food than her brother and gets a poorer standard of health care and education. She soon becomes a woman, often missing out on her adolescence. She is married early, becomes a mother soon after, and then bears more children, at intervals that are all too frequent. She has no control over any of these crucial events of her life, each of which adversely affects her health.

WILL NOBODY MARRY ME?

In a village in Gujarat, ten-year-old Meen Ben's plastic bangles jangle as her little hands scrub and wring the washing. 'I over-slept today and didn't have time to comb my hair or eat my *rotla* [wheat cake] and *saag* [cooked greens]. This happens all the time. I wish we had more time at the water-point, or I wish *Bhai* [elder brother] could bring me on his bicycle, but then he has to go to school. *Bai* [mother] says I cannot go to school, because I have to stitch and embroider to prepare my dowry – otherwise no one will marry me.'

In the past few years the opportunities for women in Indian society have expanded significantly, partly as a consequence of affirmative policies by the government and positive initiatives by NGOs and other civil-society groups – but mostly as a result of years of determined advocacy, campaigning, and action for change by women themselves. However, while some are emerging as strong and confident individuals, in control of their own lives and capable of raising their voices to demand their rights, others face a very different reality. The paradox of Sita and Draupadi persists.

The 'missing' women

Despite its proximity to the national capital, Delhi, and the state capital, Jaipur, Alwar in north-east Rajasthan has stood still in time. It is a pocket of deep neglect, illiteracy, and obscurantism, where the status of women is wretchedly low, and their participation in decision-making is marginal. The rate of female literacy is 20 per cent. About 88 per cent of girls marry by the age of 19, and about 51 per cent of them have their first pregnancies between the ages of 15 and 19 years.

The sex ratio in Alwar is 832 females to every 1000 males, well below the state average of 917:1000, for reasons that become horribly obvious each year when the pre-monsoon showers prompt a major operation to de-silt the open drains of the town: buried in the black slime are aborted foetuses and mauled bodies of abandoned baby girls. The vigilant local press, quick to report these findings, is condemned by the authorities for 'sensationalising' and 'exaggerating' the story.

▶ *The birth of a baby girl is not always welcomed in Indian families. 'Son-preference' is widespread.*

But the truth is that advances in technology have led to an increase in female foeticide: ultrasound has emerged as a preferred method of sex determination, fast replacing amniocentesis. A law passed in 1994 prohibits clinics from revealing the sex of the foetus, and requires them to register and monitor all sonograph and ultrasound facilities. But the success of the legislation depends on vigilant monitoring of the clinics' activities. In Alwar, when the 19 local nursing homes and laboratories with facilities for ultrasound/sonography tests were asked to submit records of abortions and tests conducted over the last two years, only four responded.

'Son preference' is an all-India phenomenon: in virtually every region, class, and caste, the birth of a daughter is associated with the loss of family assets. The girl is in fact not considered part of the family into which she is born, but as part of the family into which she will be married. The main cause of the problem is the dowry system: the traditional practice of giving the bridegroom gifts in cash and kind, a custom which has degenerated into specific and ever-escalating demands from the boys' families. The preference for sons manifests itself in the practice of female foeticide, female infanticide, and neglect of baby girls. What happens in Alwar is just one symptom of a far greater malaise: of a society which devalues human life and dignity.

With the exception of Kerala, which has invested considerable sums in women's development, health, and education, every state has fewer women than men. Haryana and Punjab, despite their high per capita incomes, have only 861 and 874 women respectively for every 1000 men. Orissa, one of the poorest states in terms of income, has 972 women for every 1000 men. In the words of Nobel Laureate Amartya Sen, India, with its present population of almost 1.03 billion, has to account for some 32 million 'missing women'.

Rajasthan proposes to reduce its TFR (Total Fertility Rate) from 4.1 children per woman in 1997 to 2.1 in 2016. The state holds women responsible for regulating the family size and decisions about marriage, despite the fact that most women have little say in such matters. Surgical selection of male children is not only licensed by social approval, but it is also encouraged by the State Population Policy, which rewards small families and thus reduces the survival chances of daughters.

▼ Rhudmal Meena with his wife Laxmi in Hamirpur village, Rajasthan. 'Laxmi and I have been married for 35 years. I was 9 and Laxmi was 10 when we married. In our day everyone was married off young.'

Shailan Parker/Oxfam

Women in the workforce

Nagmani is pert, capable, and literate. She lives in Pulletikurru, an extremely vulnerable village of artisans whose livelihood is threatened by floods and cyclones that strike the East Godavari Delta of Andhra Pradesh during almost every monsoon season.

Devastating floods in 1996 left Nagmani, her husband, and their two infant sons homeless and helpless. Their only source of livelihood, the pit-loom for weaving *saris* (women's traditional dress), was crushed under the collapsed roof. Nagmani recalls: 'In the first year after the disaster, some organisations helped with the repair of our loom; and in the second year they helped us to rebuild our homes. It was in the third year that I asked SAKTI [an organisation based in Hyderabad] for a loom and a small sum of working capital to buy yarn.

'All these years I could only assist my husband while he did the actual weaving. But he earned no more than a pittance, since the master weaver adjusted the price of the finished product against the yarn that he supplied and the loans that he made to us whenever we needed anything. So although my husband worked all the time, we never seemed to have enough money. Now I work and also market my products independently. Traders are happy, because they don't have to invest in me by supplying raw material and loans. For the first time I have enough money to educate my children and to pay for our health care.'

For women in India, work is far more than just a matter of survival. It was work that earned Nagmani a significant wage and built her self-esteem. Now that she is able to control her own income, work has increased her status and bargaining power within the family.

Another woman weaver

Across the country in a tiny village – Bhiansar in Rajasthan – lives Pappu. For her, work provides the only opportunity to leave the four walls of her home and meet and interact with other women. She, like Nagmani, belongs

▲ *Nagmani, a recently trained weaver: 'For the first time I have enough money to educate my children and to pay for our health care.'*

▶ *Pappu the weaver in the courtyard of her house, sitting beside her bobbin-winder*

to the *meghwal* (weaver) community, and here too, traditionally, women don't weave. They do everything else – spinning yarn and forming spindles – but not weaving. Men weave cotton fabric, and they earn the money. But that was until two years ago.

'Ganga from UMBVS [*Urmul Marusthali Bunkar Vikas Samiti*] lived here with us and changed our outlook on everything', says Pappu. 'She helped us to form a self-help group of eleven women called *Bhavna* [Aspiration]. During one of our meetings, we expressed a desire to learn weaving. Our only condition was that Jagdish Ram, from our own village, should be the trainer – otherwise the men would never allow it. I was part of the first group of seven who were taught to weave. Now I earn between Rs 1500 [£18] and Rs 2500 [£30] every month. Since my children now manage the livestock and collect fodder and fuel-wood, I am able to spend most of my time weaving.

'I couldn't even look after my own clothes when I became a mother at 15, so I could never have dreamed of weaving cloth. No woman does. The only activity that is considered to be work in this community is weaving: everything else counts for nothing. Now women even go to community meetings, and we are asked to sit right in front. Is it the money or the work that is changing our lives? I really don't know.'

Forced to work – or forbidden to work

Although Nagmani and Pappu have achieved a degree of independence through work, employment does not necessarily always improve women's situation. In India, women's seclusion within the home is often seen as a matter of social status; consequently, it is women from poor families and oppressed communities who form the bulk of the workforce. Ironically, this

▲ *The poster reads: 'Since childhood she has been kept in a cage. So how will she fly? Your daughter is in a similar predicament. Is this right?'*

association between women's seclusion and privileged social status has been internalised by the subordinate castes, who often pressurise their women to adopt upper-caste norms if they become prosperous. This was the case in Punjab during the 'Green Revolution' in the 1960s, when agricultural yields increased as a result of better seeds, fertilisers, and mechanical farming methods: women's participation in the workforce actually declined instead of increasing, as economic prosperity grew.

According to official statistics, 92.5 per cent of India's total labour force works in the informal sector, and nearly half of these workers are women. Of the total female workforce, 96 per cent is employed in the informal sector, engaged in the most insecure, poorly paid, and often most physically demanding work. Further, because of the lack of child-care support and other social-security services, their levels of productivity remain low.

The Rural Labour Commission estimated in 1991 that there were about 20 million women doing home-based work in rural areas alone. Such women, however, are largely invisible in national statistics. Because they work at home, their labour is considered to be domestic work. In fact, during surveys, many of these women refer to themselves as 'housewives', even though they spend 14–16 hours a day earning an income.

Regardless of their sector of employment – informal, formal, agricultural, or daily paid labour – women work far longer hours than men, particularly within the poorer households, because they have to bear the extra burden of domestic responsibilities. Inevitably children are required to

▶ *This poster asks: 'Why is it that I am the one who has to do all the hard work?'*

INDIA 57

▲ *Abarishi, a widow with six children to support. 'I work as a maidservant in two houses, and I get work weeding, and I sell the grass and weeds in the market as fodder. My eldest daughters also work collecting fodder, and I join them when I have finished all my other work. I have about an hour's break from the housework, and in that time I collect cow dung and sell it. It's a really hard life, but we just about manage.'*

fetch water, collect fuel-wood and fodder, tend livestock, and do numerous other chores. This kind of child labour frees adults like Pappu to engage in more remunerative activities; but in so doing, they limit their children's educational prospects, in essence laying the foundation for continued poverty.

There is a Minimum Wage law which stipulates equal wages for equal work. But it is not enforced, and women's wages are on average 30 per cent lower than men's. There is not a single state in India where men and women are paid the same wages for equal work. Home-based workers, most of whom are women, are not entitled to social-security benefits such as child care, health insurance, and old-age pensions. While the volume and value of women's work continue to be missing from national statistics, policies formulated to manage the informal economy will restrict its activities rather than capitalise on its potential.

Violence against women

All Indian women, regardless of age, class, caste, religion, and community, are vulnerable to violence. Neither marriage, education, economic security, nor social status provides any protection. Violence against women often takes the form of arbitrary deprivation of liberty, neglect of health, denial of food, emotional cruelty, and dehumanising physical abuse. Most of these abuses go unreported, because they are tolerated by society, and because women fear the stigma created by lodging complaints with the insensitive criminal-justice system. In theory, the Indian Constitution guarantees to all Indians the right to bodily integrity, personal safety, and security. Yet government statistics indicate that violence against women is increasing, and the law is poorly enforced.

Traditionally, religious laws have governed family relations in India. The major religious communities – Hindu, Sikh, Muslim, Christian, and Parsi – have their own personal and religious laws on matters of marriage,

▲ In the poster, the woman complaining of abuse by her husband is dismissed when she goes alone to the police station. When she is supported by other women, the police have to take her complaint seriously.

divorce, succession, adoption, guardianship, and maintenance. Thus (to take a typical example) Fatima in Nagpur (Maharashtra) has been left without maintenance to sustain herself and her two daughters because she could not convincingly plead her case against allegations of infidelity. She stood cowering, covered from head to toe, in front of an all-male *sarai adalat* (community court), whose basic premise was her presumed guilt.

The personal laws of minority communities have been left untouched, in accordance with an official policy of not interfering unless the demand for change comes from within. Women's groups are actively campaigning for change, but for Fatima and thousands of women like her to able to rely on the protection of the law, it will take not only committed activists and a supportive community, but also a reformed clergy.

A ROLE MODEL FOR THE WOMEN OF KHERBRAHMA

In the village of Kherbrahma in Gujarat, Shakuntala Ben is a major celebrity and a role model. Married at 17, divorced at 18, post-graduate student at 26, she now, at the age of 37, supports dozens of families who were affected by communal violence in 2002 and depend on her for security and rehabilitation.

'I come from an upper-caste family in which women do not work. Not only have I broken this taboo, but I am the only divorcée, and the first one to travel abroad. My family was tricked into marrying me to a worthless, married man. He took me to Mumbai, where he beat me and his whole family used me as domestic labour. To the horror of my family, I returned home and refused to go back. My parents insisted that despite everything a girl's place was in her marital home, and that my four sisters would never be married because of the dishonour that I had brought upon the family. That is when I realised that many women are in similar situations – doubly victimised, with no place to go to.'

Shakuntala went on to educate herself. She got a divorce from her abusive husband and is now in the process of founding a refuge for women. She was the local contact person for an Oxfam project which offered relief and rehabilitation to victims of the recent communal violence. She says proudly, 'I have been working with *Swa Shakti*, a government scheme for women entrepreneurs, and was sent to the Netherlands and the Philippines to talk about how I changed my own life and am now changing those of others. I also educated my sisters, and now all of them have professional qualifications.'

Women's rights – the theory and the practice

Even though the Indian constitution grants women equal rights with men, the legal system continues to discriminate against them – most evidently in the laws on inheritance and divorce. Theoretically women are entitled to basic property rights; but, in practice, customary and personal laws limit women's rights to inheritance, as well as their rights to custody of their children and maintenance for themselves and their children.

Under Hindu law, sons have an independent share in ancestral property, while the daughters' portions are based on the shares owned by the father. The father can disinherit a daughter by renouncing his share. Married daughters have no right to reside in their ancestral property. Rules of succession relating to agricultural land are different from personal laws. For example, in some states, such as Uttar Pradesh, daughters are prohibited by law from owning land. Widows can usually inherit land only in the absence of male heirs – of whom, of course, there are many in India's extended family system. Under Muslim law, daughters can inherit only half the share of sons. Women usually hesitate to demand their share, because in India there is no social-security system, so in the event of widowhood, divorce, or separation, they would be dependent on their own father, brother, or other male relation.

Maintenance rights awarded to women in the case of divorce are also weak. Both Hindu and Muslim laws recognise the rights of women and children to maintenance; but in practice the money is seldom sufficient, and payment schedules are often disregarded.

Another field where women continue to be marginalised is politics. Participation of women in politics has actually declined since Independence. Despite legislation to reserve 33 per cent of the seats in the *Panchayati Raj* institutions, at the national level women's representation in Parliament is a mere 7 per cent. Since 1999 there have been several unsuccessful attempts to amend the constitution in order to reserve 33 per cent of seats in the upper and lower houses of Parliament for women.

Proof of the relevance and effectiveness of Indian women's movement is the fact that the issue of women's rights is today a central

---

BAREFOOT COUNSELLORS OF VIDARBHA

'Barefoot Counsellors' is an innovative initiative of YUVA (Youth for Unity and Voluntary Action) in response to the needs of women who have suffered from domestic violence in Vidarbha, Maharashtra. These female counsellors monitor acts of violence against women within families and help agencies to collect relevant documents and statements from witnesses. They provide counselling, guidance, and even, where appropriate, conciliation services. But most importantly, they help women to bring charges against their abusers.

It was in 1999 that YUVA established a paralegal team of 15 counsellors, aged between 25 and 55. The number has since grown to 150. They are touching the lives of 75,000 people of 200 communities in five districts. The six-month training develops volunteers' skills and knowledge about gender equity, national laws and policies, and government schemes. The volunteers work in their home areas, where they share the social background of their clients and can provide counselling close to home.

Jaitun Bi, aged 50, a Barefoot Counsellor from the first batch of 1999, says: 'We do intensive preparations for each case by collecting documentary evidence, holding discussions with all concerned, and interacting with local authorities. It is not for nothing that men in my locality are better behaved than ever before: I am ruthless!'

▲ *Women are emerging from the shadows of prejudice and superstition in India, but the pace of social change is slow.*

theme of political and development discourse. Affirmative action for women's political participation, and reviews of laws and policies to ensure women's equality, are indicators of recognition at the political level. However, the pace of social change in India is very slow. The priorities of the educated urban elite among Indian women are similar to those adopted in the developed countries, focusing on positive issues like freedom of choice and identity; but more important for the vast majority is the negative liberty of not being subjected to violence.

In response to years of sustained legal activism by the women's movement, the Supreme Court has begun to apply principles of equality when judging cases of violence against women. One example is the landmark 1997 Supreme Court Judgement on Sexual Harassment at the Workplace (Vishakha vs. State of Rajasthan), which meant that every employer would henceforth be required to provide effective complaints procedures and remedies, including the award of compensation to women victims. Judgements have also begun to apply international conventions like the Convention on the Elimination of All Forms of Discrimination Against Women (CEDAW) and the Convention on Human Rights.

The common perception of domestic violence as a 'private' issue is also changing. The government has recognised the seriousness of the problem, and the need for legislation was apparent in the proposed Bill on Domestic Violence of 2002. The views of the women's movement on the issue of domestic violence were reflected in the recommendations made to a Joint Parliamentary Committee, which accepted most of them; but, following the change in government in 2004, the Bill will have to be tabled in Parliament afresh.

Rural livelihoods: claiming rights, protecting resources

Land rights

In Biona village in Uttar Pradesh lives Har Narayan, who supports his family by working as a farm labourer on daily wages. Short, lean, and weathered beyond his 35 years, he has been an itinerant labourer ever since he dropped out of school at the age of ten. During good harvests he is able to make Rs 3000 (£35) per month, but at other times finding any work at all is difficult. Recently his wife Ghuri has found it very hard to manage on his meagre wages. She has to supplement their income by depriving the children of the milk from their only cow. Sale of the milk brings in a steady Rs 30 (approximately 35 pence) per day, enough to cover the family's expenditure on condiments and cooking oil. She also has to work very hard to collect fodder, because she has no money to buy it.

Har Narayan and Ghuri have three daughters; their youngest child, Babloo, is a son. They would have preferred the son to have been the eldest, so that he could have accompanied Har Narayan on his labouring jobs. As he gazes at little Babloo playing in the mud, the father longs for a more stable future for him, which is impossible without his own piece of land. But can he even dare to dream?

'In 1975 there was an aggressive family-planning drive. This village was especially vulnerable because we are predominantly a *chamar* community, low-caste and servile, so it was hard for us to resist the pressure. The state government offered inducements but in many cases did not honour them. My father's younger brother, Sitaram, a poor unmarried youth, was sterilised by vasectomy and in exchange was given a *patta* [land deed] for two acres of redistributed land. We never got possession of the land, because the upper castes were cultivating it, and no one had the courage to demand it from them.'

After his uncle and father died, Har Narayan was unsure how to claim what was now rightfully his. Injustice and exploitation are not new to his community: in fact he does not even view the denial of his rights as an injustice, only as an inevitable legacy of the past. *Dalits*, of whom the *chamars* form a sub-caste, constitute 16 per cent of the population of India, but they own only one per cent of the cultivable land. *Dalit* status, determined by birth, affects every dimension of an individual's life. *Dalits* generally do

▲ *Har Narayan surveys the land that is rightfully his.*

not own land and are often relegated to live in separate villages and neighbourhoods.

In May 2002, the leader of the *dalit*-dominated *Bahujan Samaj Party* (BSP), Mayawati Kumari, was sworn in as Chief Minister of Uttar Pradesh. She declared that common village land would be reduced from 5 per cent to 2 per cent of the total area of cultivable land, and the surplus would then be redistributed to landless *dalit* families. But many *dalits* are sceptical about such schemes, because they do not know how to claim their rights.

Turning rights into reality

India is a mostly rural country, with almost 75 per cent of its people living in villages. Seventeen per cent of the world's population has to subsist on just 2.4 per cent of the world's surface area, which has been farmed almost continuously for 2000 years. Since agriculture remains the primary source of subsistence and income, land rights are crucial to all farmers throughout India.

India drafted progressive land-reform legislation 40 years ago. Rents were to be regulated, and tenants were to be given greater security and ownership rights. Ceilings were imposed on the area of land that could be owned by private interests, and surplus land was to be redistributed. But the government only set out the broad guidelines: the actual legislation and implementation of the Land Ceiling Act were left to the individual states. This initiative to rationalise land holdings and reform conditions of tenure had mixed results. In many states, land owners avoided the regulations by partitioning their holdings and registering some parts in bogus names. Often, as in Har Narayan's case, land that was 'redistributed' on paper has continued to be occupied by the upper castes. This is the case whether the land in question is government wasteland (unused, uncultivated land) or 'ceiling land' (private land rendered surplus by the Land Ceiling Act).

But Har Narayan, along with many others from 30 villages in the Orai District, is now part of a movement, supported by *Samarpan Jan Kalyan Samiti*, to reap the benefits of land-reform laws. When it began to work on land development in 1995, this organisation realised that nothing was possible until issues of ownership were resolved. Since then, it has been helping landless people to gain possession of land that is rightfully theirs, and ensuring that all redistributed land is registered in the joint ownership of the farmers and their wives. By scrutinising official revenue records, it has discovered that even access to irrigation canals, roads, and water points is appropriated by influential members of the community.

Initially three villages organised themselves to co-ordinate with various government agencies to claim their entitlements. Normally unresponsive officials have been spurred into action by their persistence and motivation. Most of the settlements have been reached out of court, since otherwise the illegal occupants would have had to pay huge penalties with retrospective effect. On average, six allotments of *pattas* (registrations of plot) have been achieved every month. But while Har Narayan will soon be tilling his own land, there are many more landless people across the country who are yet to realise the possibilities that the law offers them.

Water rights

The *dhimars* of Bundelkhand in Madhya Pradesh are an inland fishing community. For centuries they have earned their livelihood from *talabs* (ponds) to which they have no secure entitlement. The region is dusty and stark, without vegetation. During the long, intense monsoon, water flows downhill into approximately 500 ponds, some tiny, some as big as one square kilometre. For the *dhimars*, the ponds are a resource that is as important as land is to peasant farmers.

Ever since he can remember, Ramu Dhimar, now 45 years old, has been getting up at 4 a.m. every day from September through to the end of April. He and the other fishermen from the Kevat community trek to their pond to sail out in *kishtis* (rowing boats) to throw in the nets. Ramu does not own his boat or net; they belong to the *Thakur* (from the rich, powerful upper caste that traditionally controls local resources), who collects the daily catch and pays Ramu Rs 30 (about 35 pence) per day. Ramu's wife Phoola too gets up early, all twelve months of the year, to fetch water and feed the family before heading for the *Thakur's* house. Here she must winnow wheat, water and feed the livestock, give oil massages to the women of the house, and wash their clothes – in fact she must do anything at all that needs to be done. She does not get paid for her services, because Ramu took a loan from the *Thakur* five years back, when Phoola fell seriously ill during the birth of their sixth child. In the afternoon Phoola, along with the wives and daughters of other fishermen, heads for the *talab* to pull out the nets and sort out the fish, according to size and variety, ready to be transported for marketing.

Despite belonging to a registered fisher-folk society which has taken the pond on lease, neither Ramu nor Phoola has any share in the profit from fish culture. Both of them work, doing everything from raising the fish from the egg stage to marketing them, but only Ramu is entitled to daily wages. They now know that this society was formed by the *Thakur* with the sole intention of getting the pond on lease from the *Panchayat* (elected village

▶ *Madhya Pradesh: members of Ramu Dhimar's fishing co-operative in Bundelkhand meet to discuss their campaign to obtain legal entitlements to local ponds.*

assembly). Once the lease was acquired, he controlled the use of the pond and the lives of the dependent fishermen and women.

In some cases where fisher folk have themselves formed societies, rich brokers (who finance and thus control the catch) have prevented them from functioning properly, forcing the fisher folk to go back to them for credit. Another problem is that the ponds dry up if not properly maintained, so fisher folk suffer loss of fish and work. In such cases not only do the societies receive no compensation, but they are also made to pay a 'tax' by borrowing from the same brokers. Ramu and Phoola and 4000 other fisher folk of Tikamgarh have rights of use and control over 500 ponds of the district, but that entitlement is only in principle, ensured by the Co-operative Act. At present half the ponds are totally silted up, and 40 per cent of the remaining ponds are in the control of the feudal powers.

Against all the odds ...

Claiming access to resources for sustainable livelihoods is a major struggle for deprived and exploited rural communities. Obstacles to the efforts of people like Har Narayan, Ramu, and Phoola are institutionalised in societies where traditional practices are rigidly prescribed. Powerful groups and individuals who feel their interests threatened by change often oppose initiatives to empower the marginalised members of the community.
But change is slowly coming. As the assembled villagers sit on their haunches, enjoying the January afternoon sun, Phoola and her friend Lachhi pull in their very first catch. They have to throw most of the fish back because they are too small, probably due to the late seeding – but then the women got the Birora *talab* registered in their collective names just three months ago.

Phoola, Lachhi, and 40 other women have leased this pond, the first time that women in Bundelkhand have achieved such a thing.

It was five years ago, supported by *Vikalp*, a local NGO, that fisher folk in Tikamgarh came together to form co-operatives to fight for their rights and to develop a scheme of collective marketing and ownership. Their initial attempts were met with violent resistance from more powerful castes; but, through sheer perseverance against all odds, many fisher folk now own fishing ponds. After securing their rights of ownership, they worked collectively to solve problems of marketing, transportation, and seed purchase; they deepened the ponds and explored the idea of setting up a hatchery.

Women of this community, although an integral part of the fishing and marketing process, continued to be exploited. 'For us nothing changed. We continued to work in upper-caste households, fetch water for them, and do menial labour', recalls Phoola. Then, encouraged by Om Prakash Rewat (the moving spirit behind *Vikalp* and – ironically – a man from the dominant caste), women started meeting to organise themselves into savings groups and discuss common concerns. They demanded the rights to own ponds and fish them, just like the men. Phoola and her group of women were the first to get a fishing pond registered in their own names. The Birora pond was created from a seasonal stream with funds from UNICEF. Women used their group savings to pay for the registration, the lease, and fish seed. Now there are seven such ponds, owned exclusively by women, with the possibility of raising and harvesting enough fish to ensure a life of prosperity with food, health care, and education for their children – but also, maybe, enough to celebrate the *Diwali* festival.

▼ *Phoola's first catch from the pond that she and other local women have succeeded in leasing*

Phoola's husband says, 'We now invite women to be part of every group. Their commitment and their attitude to marketing and savings are different. Men just can't negotiate: women manage to get a far better price for the fish. In all our meetings we ensure 50/50 attendance of women and men.' The community are now negotiating the rights to farm formerly submerged fertile land next to their pond. According to land records, this belongs to those who lease the *talab*, since it figures as part of the pond.

The feudal powers in rural Indian society perpetuate the subservience of low-caste people by blocking their access to state-sponsored programmes and welfare measures. Despite these constraints, there is growing awareness now of the possibility of a better life, a life of dignity. And poor communities are beginning to find the courage to challenge powerful individuals and institutions.

Protecting productive forests

Bhimnaiko, aged 82, though infirm, plays a vital role in the Simlibanka village of Nayagarh District in Eastern Orissa. While lying in the shade, he watches over the Bhalu Mundia forest for encroachers and poachers. Relatively new to settled cultivation, he belongs to one of the 62 tribal groups in Orissa that are primarily hunter-gatherers.

'The most indelible memory from my childhood is when the Political Agent [British administrator] rewarded my father for killing nine tigers. Later we were driven out of our own forest by the government. We were like thieves in our own land. Our community has traditionally depended on the forest for its livelihood. As the woodland has dwindled, we have taken to agriculture – but we still rely on the forest. We need the products for cultivation and for consumption.'

Bhimnaiko is one of 100 million people in India who live in and around forests; another 275 million are dependent on forests for their livelihoods. Forests account for 23 per cent of the total land of India. Orissa has a larger wooded area than the national average, and – despite having rich mineral deposits and natural resources – it is one of the poorest states. Almost half of its population lives below the poverty line, compared with the national average of 26 per cent.

It was not always so. Traditionally, forests were managed in order to meet local needs and were governed by customary rules and regulations. The woodlands flourished, and local communities prospered. But profit-driven forest-management practices, inherited from the colonial administration, alienated forest-dependent communities, eroded their customary rights, and took away their incentives to protect the forests. These priceless assets were over-exploited by the state, by industry, and by private operators. The degradation of the forests was made worse by government management systems that were insensitive to local needs, and by the ever-increasing demands of the local populations (both humans and livestock). Farmers need timber for ploughs and carts, bamboo for making huge storage drums, and fodder for cattle. Their heavy dependence on forests means that these vital resources need to be conserved and regulated. In Orissa, thanks to the inspiration provided by a movement known as 'Friends of Trees and Living Beings', woodlands have been dramatically revived by a system of community-based protection and management.

▼ *Orissa: Bhimnaiko watches out for poachers in the forest around his village.*

Without trees, no life

When a teacher in Nayagarh District enters a classroom, the students greet him by saying '*Gachha bina*...[without trees]'. And he completes the sentence for them: '... *jeevana nahi* [no life]'.

Orissa was the first state to realise the importance of people's participation in forest management. It passed a resolution recognising Village Forest Protection Committees even before the National Forest Policy came into force in 1988. But in 1993 the government set up a system called Joint Forest Management, which substantially increased the policing powers of the Forestry Department, inevitably reducing the powers of the community. The aim was to engage forest-dependent communities in forest management – without giving them ownership of the patches that they managed. After working hard to regenerate their forest, Bhimnaiko's community of 20 families was not ready to give up its ownership.

It was in 1991 that the inhabitants of Simlibanka realised that the area's proximity to major markets, the availability of cheap transport through the nearby Mahanadi waterway, and exploitative government policies were robbing them of their forest resources. They decided that long-term protection of the forest was vital and that it would have to involve everyone in the community. So they resorted to the traditional practice of *thengapalli*. *Thenga* literally means a bamboo stick. In this context the stick has been used as a symbol of the community's authority. Local people take turns to protect the forest, and each day the stick is placed in front of the house of the person who is responsible for watching out for encroachers on that particular day. If any appear, villagers unite to confront them in a demonstration of non-violent resistance.

Within two years there was a visible improvement in the tree cover in Bhalu Mundia forest. But local people had no idea how to manage their growing resources fairly and sustainably. They joined a growing body of similar communities, the *Jangal Suraksha Mahasangh* (JSM – District-level Forest Protection Federation), Nayagarh, which aimed to develop skills and share experiences and concerns.

In the first year the forest was protected from all exploitation, whether herding, grazing, or fuel-wood collection. In the second, a one-time collection of long twigs was permitted for thatching houses. In the third year, bamboo collection was allowed (for fencing and support for vegetables). In the fourth year the top portion of the hillock was opened for grazing, fuel-wood collection, and collection of *medha* (small poles used for making platforms for stacking paddy). From the sixth year onwards, controlled grazing began. In the seventh year, *thengapalli* was discontinued and two watchmen were appointed to guard the forest in place of the community volunteers. Now, with verdant, revived forests and enlightened local people, that system too has become unnecessary.

With members drawn from approximately 600 villages, JSM organises collective action to promote community forest management. By co-ordinating sporadic protection initiatives, the network has succeeded in forming commonly accepted objectives, strategies, protection mechanisms, penalty systems, and benefit schemes; and, most importantly, it has successfully challenged state policies, such as Joint Forest Management, that conflict with community interests. District authorities see the JSM in a positive light, as an ally, but state authorities see it as an adversary. Initiatives such as the JSM have now come together under the *Odisha Jangal Manch*, a networking forum which represents forest-dependent village communities in Orissa, monitoring and reviewing all programmes and policies of the government.

Fruits of the forest

With the increase in tree cover, there is also an increase in forest products – but not necessarily in the fortunes of people who are dependent upon them. Unlike Bhimnaiko, who depends on the forest for agricultural purposes, Sasi Behra in the neighbouring village of Sikrida relies on non-timber forest produce (NTFP) for consumption, trading, and livelihood. But her struggle for user rights has become a struggle for survival. At different seasons of the year, Sasi Behra collects *tamarind* (used as a condiment),

▲ *Domestic animals are banned from grazing in the forest until the tree cover has been re-established..*

▶ *This village in Bhalu Mundia Forest shows what can be achieved when a community takes action to protect its natural resources.*

▲ *A member of a women's collective in Sikrida village makes plates out of sal leaves. 'Usually we produce about 450 plates per member per day.'*

kendu (tobacco leaves), *amla* (for cosmetics), *mahua* (for the local brew), *sal* leaves (for disposable plates), and *sal* seeds (for oil and pharmaceuticals). April is the season for *sal*-leaf picking. This means picking the tender leaves from the tree, stitching them with bamboo slivers to form disposable plates, or *patals*, drying them under weights to prevent curling, and then tying them in bundles of 80, ready to be sold. After all the hard work, she is not quite sure of the rate she will get – or if her products will be bought at all, or even if she will be penalised for possession of such products, which happens often.

After 1980, when the Indian government banned the felling of forest trees, NTFP became a major source of income for forest communities in Orissa. As many as 85 items are consumed and traded by local collectors; they include roots, tubers, bamboo, manure, leaves, oil seeds, cashew nuts, and medicinal herbs. Three times as many women as men are involved in gathering NTFP items; it is women almost exclusively who process them; and twice as many women as men market them.

Traders and dealers were exploiting local collectors of raw materials such as Sasi Behra. To address this problem, in 1983 the government nationalised almost all products; but the procuring government agencies continued to rely on the commercial traders' network. And, although the Price Fixation Committee decided prices for all categories of NTFP, the information was not communicated to village-level collectors – who anyway were not familiar with standard metric measurements. Their lack of bargaining strength meant that they were just as vulnerable as ever.

The situation began to change after an administrative order was issued in 2001 in relation to the Orissa Forestry Act. For the first time a distinction was made between minor forest products (MFPs) and non-timber forest products (NTFPs). Forest products like tamarind, honey, brooms, and certain oil seeds were classified as MFPs and kept under the control of *Panchayats* (local community institutions). NTFPs were classified as either 'nationalised produces' or 'lease-bar produces'. Nationalised products like *kendu* leaves, *sal* seeds, and bamboo are directly controlled by the government. Lease-bar items are *sal* leaves, gums, resins and barks, roots and climbers with medicinal uses. These are not available for free trade, because their collection on a commercial scale would damage the forest.

For primary collectors, registration with *Panchayats* was supposed to ensure local rights to the gathering and pricing of produce. But most collectors are not yet aware of this legally sanctioned means of ensuring fair trade. Unauthorised traders are still buying produce at exploitative rates, in violation of the policy. Forest gatherers get low returns because the dealers have a hold over them, and public and private monopolies dominate the trade.

To maximise local income from NTFPs, women of Sikrida are pioneering a change. In 2002, under the leadership of Sasi Behra, 17 women formed a collective, *Maa Kalika Mahila Sangathan*. Through it they have been able to acquire product leases collectively, negotiate fair prices for their produce, and even assure a market for themselves. But most importantly, along with the village Community Forest Management committee, they have successfully lobbied for the inclusion of *sal* leaf in the MFP category, although it was originally listed in the lease-bar list.

'Before the trader arrives, we bring our produce together. Usually we produce between 450 and 480 plates per member per day. Demand peaks during May and October, when weddings take place and numerous guests have to be fed. That is when the rate goes up to Rs 12 [14 pence] per bundle. If we had storage capacity, we could ensure this price all the time', says a confident Sasi Behra. She refuses to calculate her total income, because in her belief system to talk about good fortune is to invite bad luck. Memories of selling the bundles for rates as low as Rs 3 (4 pence) or Rs 5 (6 pence) are still fresh in her mind.

An unsustainable revolution

Independent India inherited a famine-prone and drought-prone country that was highly vulnerable to the vagaries of the weather. Although India has since achieved self-sufficiency in food, the price has proved very high in social and ecological terms.

Agricultural development in India underwent a major change from the mid-1960s, when the government's policy of encouraging the use of high-yield seeds, irrigation networks, mechanised farming, and subsidised chemical fertilisers and power led to a transformation commonly referred to as 'the Green Revolution'. Farmers were guaranteed minimum prices for their food-grain crops, as an extra impetus to increase their production. Between 1960 and 1990, India's wheat production tripled, irrigated areas increased by 60 per cent, fertiliser consumption grew ten-fold, and the installation of irrigation pumps increased twenty-fold.

But the Green Revolution could not produce more from the available resources of land, water, and labour without doing either ecological harm or social damage – or both. Over-exploitation of ground water for irrigation has resulted in severe water shortages. The water table has gone down in many parts of the country. Thirty-six per cent of irrigated land is damaged – rendered waterlogged, or too alkaline or too saline for cultivation. Intensive production without conserving the fertility and structure of the soil has led to increasing desertification and soil erosion. Chemical fertilisers have contributed to the toxicity of soil and crops.

Marginal farmers could not afford the technology-based inputs on which the Green Revolution was founded. It was rich land owners who appropriated most of the benefits, while the landless and marginal farmers remained in poverty. In national terms, India had become self-sufficient in

▲ *Babi Ben and her husband own land in Gujarat, but a seven-year drought has prevented them from growing crops. They work with their sons in the Kanoria salt works. 'We come out here at midnight and work until 9 am; after that it's too hot and the sun's too bright for working. Look at me! This is my life. Young turns old in the salt pans.'*

▶ *Rajasthan: the Aravari River disappeared in 1985, dried up by continued droughts. Now, thanks to water-harvesting and tree-planting schemes, the river flows all year round.*

food, but the problem of poverty in the villages remained unresolved. Furthermore, neglect of indigenous and traditional systems of managing water, forests, and land has made it impossible to ensure a continuous flow of sustainable production. There is a growing realisation that for sustainable development, the needs of the present have to be met without compromising the ability of future generations to meet their own needs.

Traditional solutions: water harvesting in Alwar

During the drought of 1985, as many as four members of each family were migrating from the villages in Alwar District of Rajasthan to find work elsewhere. Then *Tarun Bharat Sangh* (TBS), a newly established voluntary organisation with a team of dedicated fieldworkers, initiated a relief scheme and identified the neglect of a tradition that had sustained Alwar and its populace for centuries.

Large-scale deforestation and mining-related activities in the District had ruined the serene landscape and led to severe soil erosion. Failure of government interventions caused further decline in the area, prompting the government of Rajasthan to declare a 'dark zone' – an area where the water table had receded below recoupable level. TBS, inspired by a tradition that was fading away, organised villagers from eight administrative blocks in Alwar to erect water tanks, or *johads*. Surrounded by earthen walls, designed to maximise the conservation of rainwater, the *johads* transformed the ecology, agriculture, economics, and general well-being of the population of several villages here.

▲ *A johad constructed by TBS in Gopalpura village, Rajasthan. The three-sided dam collects water during the monsoon; the fourth side is open to allow water to cover as much land as possible. The open side also allows access for cattle – and for the village children, who use the johad as a swimming-pool.*

Check dams were built to prevent erosion, and *nalahs* (drains) were dug to supply over-flow from the *johads* to the villagers for irrigating their fields. The villagers pledged to stop cutting wood and grazing their animals in the catchment of the check dam, so that erosion could be reduced. Soon agricultural yields increased, and agricultural residue was available as a substitute for fodder previously collected from the catchment areas. Livestock-dependent landless households, who were severely affected by the grazing ban, were given shares in the irrigation water, which they could barter. Villagers had exclusive rights to the produce of the trees that were planted in the catchment areas. These dramatic ecological and economic gains soon came to be recognised as a successful model of fair and participatory resource management. And in recognition of his contribution, Rajinder Singh, the initiator of TBS, was awarded the Ramon Magsaysay Award (a Philippine government award for innovative service to humanity) in 2001.

Indian villages get most of their rain as a heavy monsoon downpour for just 100 hours out of the total 8760 hours in a year. Since most of India's agriculture is rain-fed, there exists a rich tradition of water harvesting.

People in each region have evolved their own techniques, in keeping with the local geo-climatic zones. Rajinder Singh proved beyond doubt that not only are these methods more enduring than sophisticated hi-tech measures, but they promote the survival of rural livelihoods.

'Water is our identity'

Sukhpur is the archetypal village of the drought-prone Kutch district of Gujarat, which of all the world's deserts has the highest density of human and animal populations. As he reflects upon his mixed fortunes, 40-year-old Kanha Bhai recalls a local saying: 'In one century there are seven famines, 27 years of plenty, and 63 moderate drought years; the remaining three are disastrous drought years'.

This is the fifth consecutive year of drought, and for the first time even the village pond is dry. Along with 60 others on a food-for-work scheme, Kanha Bhai is strengthening the mud wall around the village pond, to collect water when it flows in during the next rainfall. This would provide water for irrigation and livestock. The pond fell into disuse when various government schemes for piped water reached the village. Even at the best of times these were inadequate, but now they have been dry for the past three years.

In the middle of the dry pond is a raised structure that is the village well, sited here to permit filtered recharge (through the wall of the well) from the surrounding water. The village is proud of this well, which is the only one for miles that continues to provide potable water, since being restored to its present mint condition. 'Water is our identity – we have it, we are blessed. We don't have it, we are destitute', asserts Kanha. This well too will soon dry up, but everyone in Sukhpur prefers to talk about the here and now.

Kanha and his companions are labouring to revive a traditional water system that had fallen into disrepair. The decision to initiate this work was taken by the village elders, with technical and financial support from Cohesion, a group which has initiated natural-resource management projects in the district and has already restored 25 such village ponds. The impact of this initial input will be visible only after a rainfall, but meanwhile the scheme is providing much-needed food and employment to one person per family from a population of 2500. And if the drought persists, *bunds* (low earth walls) will be built around individual farmlands to stop the erosion of their soil by wind.

▼ *Women drawing water from the well in Sukhpur, Gujarat*

Shailan Parker/Oxfam

So far Kanha's family of five has been subsisting on wages from salt panning in the salt farms (Rs 5 for 100 kg) just a few kilometres away. Their two cows are in the *Panjara Pol*, to be reclaimed whenever they are able to feed them. *Panjara Pol* is a traditional collective cattle-care system, supported by donations of money, fodder, and land to protect the holy cow during drought.

For Kanha, farm-land size is not an issue, since even the poorest farmer here has large holdings, up to 25 acres. The problem is output. In former years, a mixture of any four seeds was sown, so that at least some could be harvested, depending on the fickle weather conditions. Traditional practices of cultivation and storage could usually cope with the impact of the recurring droughts. One good harvest sustained the family for up to three years and also took care of the seeds, while fodder and firewood were by-products of the crops. During the last few years, Kanha Bhai has been cultivating *jojo* and *senna*, which are in great demand for medicinal purposes. The profits were initially good, but fluctuations in price have created problems for him. And all the while his soil is becoming more saline. He knows that not all his problems will be solved by just one rainfall – despite the fact that Sukhpur literally means 'land of contentment'.

The National Water Policy

India's new National Water Policy (2002), intended to resolve problems created by successive droughts and water scarcity, ignores all the recent successes of community water-management strategies and instead emphasises central government control over water resources. The new policy also ignores the potential benefits of rainwater harvesting and the importance of involving local communities in simple methods to ensure that rainwater is trapped and refills natural aquifers in the ground.

In fact, in keeping with the global trend to make water a commodity, the NWP has encouraged private business interests to participate in 'building, owning, operating, easing and transferring of water resources facilities'. Moreover, ten-year tax holidays have been announced for investors and implementing agencies, to boost the involvement of the private sector. This is despite the Prime Minister's statement on 31 May 2002 that the NWP should be people-centred and should recognise communities as the 'rightful custodians of water'. But this commitment is contradicted in the NWP, which requires all states to frame privatisation policies within two years.

NGOs that promote community management of natural resources see a ray of hope in the 73rd amendment of the constitution. This measure transferred sufficient powers to the *Panchayats* to take control of local water, land, and natural resources. There is scope for policies on water to be developed from the *Panchayat* upwards, rather than from the top downwards. Community management systems like those in Alwar and Sukhpur have proved that equitable access to water plays an essential role in sustainable development, and such schemes deserve to be replicated.

'My granny goes out to work'

Female scarecrows, a rarity anywhere else, are a common sight in Kelia, a predominantly *dalit* village in Jalaun District of Uttar Pradesh. Their presence is explained by the remarkable achievements of the women of this community.

Girija Devi is the lively and talkative president of the Watershed Programme, *Jalagam Vikas Mandal*, ably assisted by the treasurer, Munni, and a committee of eleven women. 'I was very different in 1995, when I first met the people from *Samarpan* [a local organisation]. In fact we were all very suspicious of them. We watched them from inside our houses, but we refused to come out. Then one day they organised a race for women. We had to run with brass pots on our heads, and they were giving away these pots as prizes. This was a very attractive proposition, so Munni and I decided to join in. Despite not being able to see clearly, with my head and face covered, I won a prize. That was how I got the courage to attend their meetings.

'We formed a grain bank and then slowly, in groups of 15, started saving small amounts of money. Until then we were exploited by money-lenders, who were our only source of support during difficult times. They not only charged huge interest but treated us like bonded labour and even demanded a share of our crop.

'As the collective savings grew, we met to take decisions about our money and tackle problems that affected all of us. This was when we all decided to stop covering our faces. Initially there was resistance from our men, but we overcame this by including them in our meetings. Prosperity is attractive: our success encouraged more women to join.

'My self-help group leased land in our names, decided about cultivation and disposal of the crops, and even kept the profit in our own names. We are so different now: we are confident, we have a voice, and we know how to deal with *babus* [state officials]. For example, Munni was slow to repay her government loan, so one day a policeman came to take her to the police station. But she said she would not go until they gave her the summons in writing and sent a policewoman to accompany her. In earlier times we were too shy to even look at people in the face.

'Last year the villagers decided that a trap was needed to redirect water from the minor canal to irrigate a large tract of fallow land. The district authorities estimated the cost at Rs 50,000 [about £600], way beyond their budget. Since we had a cohesive, successful committee, they approached us – almost as a challenge. We agreed to do it, but only after our demand was met: every one in the village should contribute, either in cash or with labour.

'We completed the de-silting of the minor canal and construction of the slide-trap in eight days, at an expense of Rs 22,000 [approximately £260]. It irrigates 110 hectares and has benefited 79 families. People used to say "*nari Bharat nahin leepti*" [women cannot be builders of India]. Do they believe it now? I feel very proud when my grand-daughter says "*Dadi duty par jave hai*" [My granny goes out to work].'

Securing the future

As I travelled across India, visiting communities to gather background information for this book, it was pride and confidence that I encountered, seldom despair. Chhota, a disabled woman in drought-ridden Mortuka Dhani (Rajasthan), insists on being included in the muster roll of the government's 'food for work' programme: despite her restricted mobility – the result of polio – she confidently demands her entitlement. Bhavna Patel of Indore (Madhya Pradesh), encouraged by the organisation *Deen Bandhu Samajik Sanstha* (DBSS), knows it is her right to demand alternative housing before abandoning her tenancy in the slums of Indore. Arjunji Gujjar, aged 80, of *Tarun Bharat Sangh* in Thanagazi, is nonchalant as he recounts his moment in history: he received an award from the President of India on behalf of his community in 2001, for bringing water back to a dried-up river bed.

But the fact remains that the lives of Chhota, Bhavna Patel, Arjunji Gujjar, and millions like them are defined by poverty – poverty which increases their vulnerability to disease, crop failures, unemployment, domestic violence, and natural disaster. All such events hit the poor particularly hard and threaten to push them into destitution.

Poverty reduction and agricultural development were central themes of the founders of modern India. Since then, social indicators have improved: literacy rates continue to rise, and infant mortality continues to decline. Life expectancy at birth has increased, as has school enrolment. Gaps between male and female access to social services are narrowing. Famines and severe epidemics have been all but eliminated. The country's vibrant democracy and free press have been major factors in these achievements.

▲ *Chhota, who demanded work despite her disability*

▶ *Arjunji Gujjar, who received an award from the President of India for bringing water back to a dried-up river bed*

But Indian poverty is undeniable, and it remains both a moral issue and a political embarrassment.

India has more scientists, engineers, and technicians than most countries in the world; but while their achievements at home are contributing to developments abroad, Indian systems remain archaic and inefficient. Historical circumstances are partly to blame, but the problem is mostly attributable to failures of national leadership. Indian-developed software is widely used in the world's banks – but Indian banks cannot take advantage of it. Indian-developed management systems are used in ports and terminals around the world to speed up shipments and increase reliability, but India's own infrastructure is chronically inefficient. Ironically, Indian soldiers who fought against the Pakistan army in the frozen heights of Kargil in 1999 were equipped with obsolete field telephones, while the Pakistanis had sophisticated satellite phones, based on technology developed by Indian software engineers and programmers in the West. The trend began some 1500 years ago: it was Indian mathematicians who created the decimal system, which was carried to Baghdad and eventually passed to the West, where it replaced roman numerals.

India's undoubted potential to benefit all of its people remains relatively untapped. There is increasing evidence that whether the issue is forestry, irrigation, rural roads, urban sanitation, credit facilities, or drinking water, local communities have proved themselves able partners who make wise decisions and protect their communal and private investments with a care and vigilance that far surpass those of any government agency. But government institutions have been slow to respond to social changes: the lower castes' assertion of their rights, the gradual empowerment of women, growing social and political awareness, and the demand for a progressive polity and administration, offering a fairer share of the fruits of development.

▼ *Gujarat: Himi Ben, aged 19: 'Life is hard here because of the drought. Before that there was the cyclone, and then the earthquake. I am on the village committee. People tell us about their problems, and we suggest how to make things better. The big problem was unemployment, but through Oxfam we got work and now we can earn our living.'*

Chhota, Bhavna Patel, and Arjunji Gujjar consider the various official institutions that touch their lives to be important but ineffective. While expressing appreciation for government programmes, they maintain that many public services and programmes suffer from corrupt governance and weak accountability. The Association of Workers and Peasants (*Mazdoor Kisan Shakti Sangathan*), led by the social activist Aruna Roy, attempted to confront this very issue. When the MKSS demanded transparency in rural development expenditures in the year 2000, it was met with resistance by the government of Rajasthan. But today the state accepts that citizens have a right to information and it has even enacted pioneering legislation to ensure it. Now, all over Rajasthan, government offices list and display details of the development works being undertaken by various departments, and they are required to produce on demand employment registers and details of people to whom contracts have been awarded. It is a start, but much ground still needs to be covered.

For most people in India, well-being signifies work that is stable and safe, food for the family regardless of the year's rainfall or the morning's catch at sea, and a surplus to rely on. They remain hopeful, and they have the will to work to fulfil their aspirations for a better and fuller life. There is a growing realisation that India's great problem is not poor people, but poverty, and that those who should be consulted about ways of reducing poverty are poor people themselves.

▲ Selling coconuts on the street in Kolkata. Coconut water is more refreshing than sweet, fizzy drinks. Because it is sterile, and contains exactly the right balance of salts and sugars, it is often used to rehydrate babies in hospital.

India: facts and figures

Capital
New Delhi

Official language
Hindi

Land area
3,287,263 sq km (the sixth largest country in the world)

Population (2001 census)
1.027 billion (the second largest in the world)

Density of population
324 per sq km (average)

Population growth (1991–2001)
21.34%

Main cities (population in millions, 2001 census)
Mumbai (Bombay) 16.4; Kolkata (Calcutta) 13.2; Delhi 12.8; Chennai (Madras) 6.4; Bangalore (5.7); Hyderabad 5.5

Religions
Hinduism (83%); Islam (11%); Christianity (2.3%); Sikhism (1.9%); Buddhism (0.8%); Jainism (0.4%)

Life expectancy
64 years (male) and 65 years (female)

Sex ratio
933 females per 1000 males
(927 females per 1000 males in the 0–6 age group)

Literacy
65 per cent (males 76 per cent; females 54 per cent)

Infant mortality
72 per 1000 live births

Maternal mortality
437 per 100,000 live births

Rural population
72 per cent

Poverty
26 per cent live below the official poverty line

Agriculture
64 per cent of total work force
26 per cent of gross domestic product
18 per cent of India's exports

Currency (August 2004)
85 Indian Rupees = £1
46 Indian Rupees = $1

Per capita income (annual)
Rs 16,486 (£194)

Foreign trade
Exports $44 billion; imports $50 billion

India's share in world trade
0.7 per cent

UNDP Human Development Index Ranking
124th place among 173 nations

Dates and events

Some landmarks in the development of modern India

1526 Babur founds the Mughal empire, with its capital in Agra.

1612 British East India Company establishes trading post at Surat in Gujarat.

1798 Company troops begin military campaigns to subdue Indian territories.

1799 Fourth Mysore War ends in victory for the British.

1818 East India Company gains virtual control of India.

1853 First railway line opened in India, from Bombay to Thane.

1857 Indian Mutiny (First War of Independence).

1858 British crown assumes direct governance of India.

1885 Foundation of Indian National Congress.

1906 Foundation of Muslim League.

1919 Jallianwala Bagh massacre of demonstrators at Amritsar.

1920 Indian Congress launches campaign of non-violent resistance to British rule, inspired by Mohandas K. Gandhi.

1929 Resolution of Independence passed at Lahore congress.

1947 India partitioned: creation of Pakistan (East and West). India achieves independence.

1948 Mahatma Gandhi assassinated. Kashmir accedes to union with India.

1950 India becomes a Republic (26 January).

1951 First Five Year Plan inaugurated.

1964 Death of Prime Minister Nehru.

1965 Hostilities with Pakistan over Kashmir. Hindi proclaimed national language.

1966 Nehru's daughter, Indira Gandhi (Congress Party), becomes Prime Minister.

1971 Second Indo-Pakistan War. India recognises new State of Bangladesh (formerly East Pakistan).

1974 India becomes sixth nuclear power by exploding nuclear device.

1975 Declaration of Emergency, in response to 'internal disturbance', drastically curtails political and individual rights.

1983 India's multi-purpose satellite, INSAT-1B, successfully blasts off aboard space shuttle 'Challenger' from Cape Canaveral, USA.

1984 Indian troops enter Golden Temple in Amritsar to evict militant Sikhs. Indira Gandhi assassinated by Sikh bodyguards; succeeded as Prime Minister by her son, Rajiv Gandhi. Bhopal disaster: several thousand people die in major industrial accident.

1990 Renewed violence in Jammu and Kashmir; Governor's rule imposed.

1991 Former Prime Minister Rajiv Gandhi assassinated by a member of the Tamil liberation movement.

1992 Increasing popular support for Hindu nationalist BJP. Hindu militants destroy Babri Masjid mosque in Ayodhya; widespread communal riots ensue.

1998 BJP victory in parliamentary elections. Atal Behari Vajpayee sworn in as Prime Minister. India conducts nuclear tests, prompting similar tests by Pakistan.

2004 BJP defeated in parliamentary elections. Manmohan Singh (Congress Party) is sworn in as Prime Minister, leading the United Progressive Alliance.

▼ *The Golden Fort of Jaisalmer, Rajasthan*

Sources and further reading

Maya Chadda *Ethnicity, Security and Separatism in India* (Oxford University Press, 1997)

Stephen P. Cohen *India – Emerging Power* (Oxford University Press, 2003)

Tim Dyson et al. *Twenty-First Century India* (Oxford University Press, 2004)

Joe Human and Manoj Pattanaik *Community Forest Management: A Casebook from India* (Oxfam GB, 2000)

Indira Gandhi Institute of Development Research *India Development Report 2002*

Government of India *Economic Survey 2001–2002*

Government of India *India 2003: A Reference Manual*

N.K. Jain *Report of the Eleventh Finance Commission for 2000–2005*

Niraja Gopal Jayal *Democracy in India* (Oxford University Press, 2001)

Sunil Khilnani *The Idea of India* (Penguin, 1999)

Prem Kirpal *Culture and Development* (Har Anand, 1993)

K.M. Mathew *Manorama Yearbook 2003*

R.K. Pachauri and F. Lubina Qureshy *Population, Environment and Development* (Vikas, 1997)

K.N. Panikkar *The Concerned Indian's Guide to Communalism* (Viking, 1999)

Manoj Rai et al. *The State of Panchayat: A Participatory Perspective* (PRIA, 2001)

Mira Seth *Women and Development: The Indian Experience* (Sage, 2001)

K.L. Sharma *Social Inequality in India: Profiles of Caste, Class and Social Mobility* (Sage, 1999)

Guy Sorman *The Genius of India* (Macmillan, 2001)

S. Subramanian *India's Development Experience* (2001)

UNFPA *India: Programme Review and Strategic Development*

Ashutosh Varshney and Jeffrey Sachs (eds.) *India in the Era of Economic Reforms* (Oxford University Press, 2000)

Acknowledgements

Writers know more than anyone else that books are never written alone; and that during the process, someone who contributed an essential insight might fade into the fabric of the narrative. I am indebted to all whom I met during the course of researching this book, for giving and sharing so generously of their time, insights, hospitality, and resources. The experience was both enriching and humbling.

I wish to thank Biranchi Upadhyay for his initial guidance; it was his support that galvanised the project. I am especially grateful to Aditi Kapoor for her patience as she plodded through early drafts, cheerfully balancing 'the micro and the macro'. Her faith in me gave me strength beyond the writing. Dr N.C. Saxena and Siddo Deva contributed helpful comments on early drafts. Shailan Parker's was the sensitive eye that enriched the project – and he was the perfect travelling companion, with the profoundly telling philosophy: 'Up to you'.

And I am indebted to the teams at the various Oxfam offices, for making it all possible.

Pamela Bhagat

◀ *A primary school class, Hyderabad*

▶ *Village musicians playing traditional instruments*

Oxfam GB in India

Jonathan Ransford/Oxfam

For more than 50 years Oxfam Great Britain has been part of the dynamics of change in India, participating in the nation's progress, while sharing its concerns about persistent poverty, inadequate public services, communal conflicts, natural disasters, and the deterioration of natural resources.

Oxfam in India is responding to these challenges through three main programmes, which support sustainable livelihoods, help communities to prepare for and respond to disasters, and promote gender equality. Four pilot programmes focus on urban poverty, minority girls' education, reduction of communal conflict, and HIV/AIDS. Oxfam's work links grassroots development initiatives with high-level advocacy to influence public policy and achieve lasting change. Oxfam works on development programmes in ten states but responds to crises, as appropriate, in any part of the country.

Oxfam's commitment to listening and learning from the grassroots and its practice of engaging in debate with policy makers give it access to information at all levels. This is apparent in the types of partner that Oxfam works with: a disaster-response and advocacy group in Wirepetta; in Nagaland, an organisation that integrates people living with HIV/AIDS into society; in Lucknow, a resource centre for a campaign to claim constitutional rights on behalf of women; in Jodhpur, a group that helps *dalits* to challenge discrimination; in Rapar, a natural-resource management programme; and 250 other organisations across the country. In the past, many partnerships that began with their first small grant from Oxfam, like *ANAND, UMBVS (Urmul Marusthali Bunkar Vikas Samiti)*, and *Tarun Bharat Sangh*, have received international recognition for their work with poor communities.

Oxfam recognises the power of civil-society institutions to influence development policy and practice in India. It works with other elements of civil society to ensure that the interests of poor people are placed at the heart of policy and practice in matters such as conflict resolution, forest management, rights over resources for secure livelihoods, and market access for small producers. Oxfam's long history of working in India means that it has rich institutional experience on which to draw in the search for effective and creative approaches to the challenges of poverty and suffering.

Oxfam's resources are modest compared with the problems that it seeks to address. Its funds are managed under two heads. 'Restricted' funds are given by specific donors for special programmes agreed in consultation with the donor. During emergencies these monies may rise to £4 million. 'Unrestricted' funds are a general pool of funds raised as donations from individuals and organisations. These funds can be used for any programmatic and administrative work. In the budgets for the year 2004–05, the unrestricted funds are £1,991,999 and restricted funds are £2,090,000.

◀ *Earthquake response, 2001: unloading Oxfam water and sanitation equipment at Ahmedabad airport*

▼ *Kilolai Naadi in drought-ridden Rajasthan: women collecting water from a pond constructed by a local NGO, with Oxfam support*

Oxfam's head office in New Delhi is supported by four regional offices in Lucknow, Ahmedabad, Hyderabad, and Kolkata; it co-ordinates programmes spread over the whole country. In early 2004, the South Asia regional office of Oxfam GB moved from Dhaka in Bangladesh to New Delhi, in view of the strategic position that India occupies in the region and increasingly on the international stage. The dynamics of change continue within Oxfam too.

Shailan Parker/Oxfam

Index

abortions 53–4
administration
   inadequacies of 10, 37, 79
   see also infrastructure; Ministry of Human Resource Development
Agreement on Textiles and Clothing 41
agricultural development 57, 71–6
   see also land rights; rural development; water rights
Ahmedabad 17, 18, 32
AIDS 43, 49–51
Alwar 53–4, 72
Andhra Pradesh 32, 46, 54
animism 16
architecture 22–3, 24
arsenic poisoning 48
arts 24–6
Arunachal Pradesh 10, 15, 16
Assam 10
Ayodhya (Babri) Mosque 7–8, 17, 83

Bada Gobindpur village 49–50
Bangladesh 12, 18, 82
Barefoot Counsellors 60
Behra, Sasi 69–71
Bhartiya Janata Party 8, 83
Bhiansar village 26, 55–6
Bihar 43, 46
Biona village 62–4
birth attendants 46
birth rates 28–9, 43
   see also childbirth
border regions
   problems in 12–13
   see also Kashmir
British rule 5–6, 20, 24, 82
Buddhism 3, 4, 15
Bundelkhand 64–6

caste 11, 19–21, 46
   see also dalits; *meghwal* weavers
Chacha village 39
child labour 57–8
childbirth 46–7
   see also birth rates
Christianity 16
civil service *see* administration
Cohesion 74
colonisation *see* British rule
communal violence 7–8, 16–18, 83
communalism 6, 7, 18
constitution 9, 10, 14
   and caste 20
   development of 7, 11, 75
   and education 45
   and women 60
crafts 24–6
culture 24–7
   and population trends 29–30
   see also religion
cyclones 38

dai (birth attendants) 46
dalits, status of 11, 20, 62–3
daughters *see* girls
death rates 28, 29, 30, 43, 47, 53, 81
debt, levels of 35
Deen Bandhu Samajik Sanstha (DBSS) 33, 77
Delhi 2, 4, 31, 32
Devi, Girija 76
disasters
   preparation for 38–9
   see also earthquake
divorce laws 60
domestic violence 58–60, 61
dowry system 54

earthquake, Gujarat 2, 37–8, 39
East Pakistan *see* Bangladesh
economic conditions 35–6, 81
   see also textile industry
economic development 32
   government policies 12, 34–5, 36–7
   for slum dwellers 33
   and the textile industry 41
   see also agricultural development; rural development
education 44–6
   and population control 29, 30
   statistics 43, 45, 53, 81
   see also sex education
elections 7, 8, 83
Emergency, State of (1975–77) 7, 82
eviction, fight against 32–3

family planning 29–30
farming *see* agricultural development; fish culture; land rights
federal structure 9–10
fish culture 64–6
forest management 67–71

Gandhi, Indira 7, 82
Gandhi, Mohandas Karamchand 6, 9, 14, 21, 82
Gandhi, Rajiv 7, 82, 83
girls
   education for 44–5
   status of 53–4
Girls' Camp programme 45
globalisation 41–2
governments 7, 8, 82, 83
   AIDS policy 50–51
   economic policies 12, 34–5, 36–7
   forestry policies 67, 68, 70
   population policy 29

water policy 75
see also administration; federal structure; local government; Ministry of Human Resource Development; State of Emergency
Green Revolution 57, 71–2
Gujarat
  earthquake 2, 37–8, 39
  population 15, 30
  water system in 74–5
  see also Ahmedabad

Hangia Vand village 37
harijans see scheduled castes
Haryana 30, 37, 54
health 43, 46–7, 49–51
health care 47–9, 51
Hinduism 3, 4, 6, 14–15, 16, 60
  see also Bhartiya Janata Party; caste
Hindus, conflicts with Muslims 7–8, 17–18
HIV/AIDS 43, 49–51
hospitals 48–9
housing rights
  for slum dwellers 32–3
  see also land rights

immunisation 47
India
  as a British colony 5–6, 20, 24, 82
  conflicts with Pakistan 13, 82
  early history 3–5, 82
  federal structure 9–10
  independence 6–9, 82–3
  statistics 81
  see also border regions; constitution; governments
Indian National Congress 6, 82
Indore, slums in 32–3
infant mortality 29, 30, 43, 53, 81
infrastructure
  inadequacies of 32, 78
  see also administration
inheritance laws, and women 60
Ishanapur 38
Islam 4, 6, 13, 15, 16, 60
  see also Ayodhya (Babri) Mosque; Muslims

Jainism 15
Jalagam Vikas Mandal 76
Jangal Suraksha Mahasangh (JSM) 68–9
jati see caste
judicial system
  inadequacies of 10, 59
  see also divorce laws; inheritance laws

Karnataka 12, 32
Kashmir 12, 13, 16, 17, 82, 83
Kelia village 76
Kerala 12, 16, 30, 43, 46, 54
Kherbrahma village 59
Kolkata 5, 31, 32, 48
Kumar, Sanjay 49–50

labour force *see* child labour; women; workforce
Lakshadweep 16
land rights 62–4
  see also housing rights
language 24
legal system *see* judicial system
literacy *see* education
literature 25
local government 11–12

Maa Kalika Mahila Sangathan 71
Madhya Pradesh 18, 32, 46, 64
Maharashtra 15, 32
markets *see* trade
marriage 52, 53, 54, 59
maternal mortality 29, 43, 47
Mazdoor Kisan Shakti Sangathan (MKSS) 79
Meghalaya 16, 46
meghwal weavers 39–40, 55–6
migration, to towns 31–3
Ministry of Human Resource Development 43
mortality *see* death rates
Mumbai 31, 32
Muslims
  conflicts with Hindus 7–8, 17–18
  see also Islam

Nagaland 10, 16
National Population Policy 29
National Water Policy 75
Nehru, Jawaharlal 7, 14, 24, 34, 82
non-timber forest produce 69–71
nuclear weapons 8, 13, 82, 83

Odisha Jangal Manch 69
Orissa 23, 35, 37, 38–9, 49–50, 54, 67–1
Oxfam 18, 37, 86–7

Pakistan 6, 13, 18, 82
  see also Bangladesh
Panchayati Raj Institutions 11–2, 46, 60, 75
performing arts 24–5
political parties 7
  see also Bhartiya Janata Party
politics, women in 11, 12, 60
population trends 28–30, 43, 53, 54, 81
  see also urbanisation
poverty 36–7, 77–9
  statistics 35, 37, 43, 81
  see also rural development; slums
PRIs 11–12, 46, 60, 75
protectionism 41
Pulletikurru village 55–6
Punjab 10, 12, 16, 30, 54, 57

Rajasthan 22, 26, 32, 39–40, 46, 53–4, 72–4, 79
Ram, Revata 39–40
Rambagh village 45
Ramdev Peer Vand village 45
religion 14–16, 81
  conflicts 7–8, 17, 82, 83
  freedom of 14
  politicisation of 16–19
  see also Buddhism; Christianity; Hinduism; Islam; Jainism; Sikhism; Zoroastrianism
rights *see* housing rights; land rights; water rights; women, rights
rural development 11–12, 37–8, 39–40
  see also agricultural development; forest management; land rights; textile industry; water rights

Sahu, Sumati 49
Samarpan Jan Kalyan Samiti 63–4, 76
scheduled castes 11, 21
secularism 14
self-help groups 33, 56, 65–6, 76
sex education 49–50
Sikhism 6, 16
Sikkim 15
Sikrida village 69–70
Simlibanka village 67–8
Singh, Manmohan 8, 83

INDIA 89

slums 31, 32-3
social security benefits 33, 58, 60
State of Emergency (1975–77) 7, 82
subsidies, failure of 35, 37
Sukhpur village 74-5
Surya Dev Nagar 32-3

Tamil Nadu 15, 23, 30
Tarun Bharat Sangh (TBS) 72–3, 77, 87
terrorism 10
textile industry 39–41, 55-6
trade
   development of 40–42
   in forest products 69–71
   statistics 81
tribal people *see dalits*

Urmul Marusthali Bunkar Vikas Samiti (UMBVS) 39–40, 56, 87
urbanisation 31-3, 36
Uttari Rajasthan Milk Union Limited (URMUL) 39–40, 45, 46
Uttar Pradesh 18, 46, 60, 62-4, 76
   see also Ayodhya

Vikalp 66
violence
   against women 58–60, 61
   communal 7–8, 16–18, 83
Vishwa Yuva Kendra (VYK) 49

Wag, Asha 32-3
wages 58
water harvesting 72-5
water rights 64–6, 75
water supplies, inequality of 32
weaving *see* textile industry
welfare benefits 33, 58, 60
women
   health 46-7
   in politics 11, 12, 60
   rights of 9, 60–61
   seclusion of 56-7
   self-help groups 33, 56, 65–6, 76
   social security benefits 33, 58, 60
   statistics 53, 54, 57
   status 9, 29–30, 52–, 66
   violence against 58–60, 61
   wages 58
   as workers 55–6, 57–8, 59, 64, 65–6, 76
   see also girls
workforce, statistics 57
World Trade Organisation 41–2

Zoroastrianism 16

▶ *Mohammad Shakeel helps his mother to prepare the family's evening meal at their home in Hyderabad.*

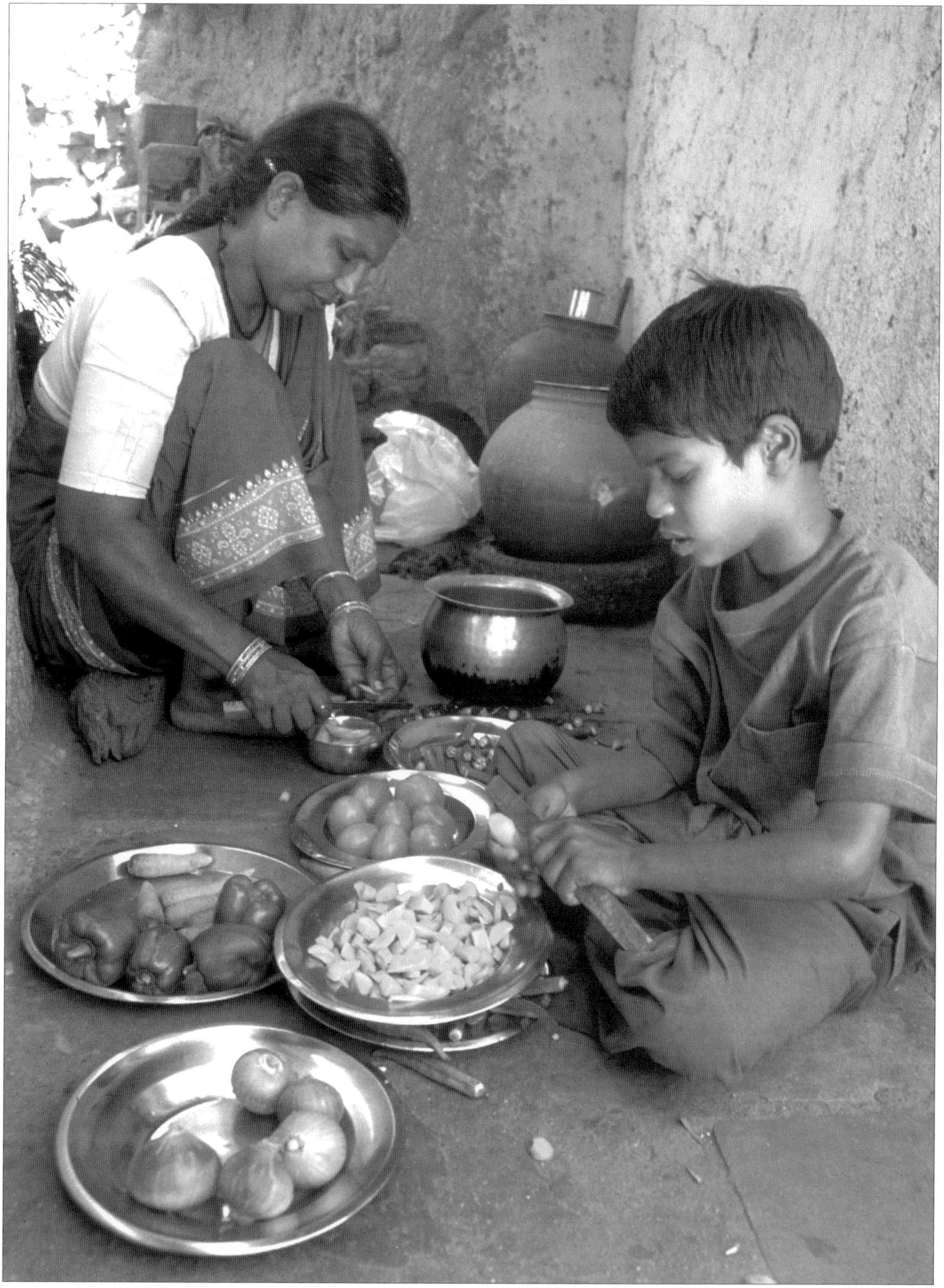

Rajendra Shaw/Oxfam